# James Joyce

# JAMES JOYCE

## *A Critical Introduction*

HARRY LEVIN

FABER AND FABER
3 Queen Square
London

First published in 1944
by Faber and Faber Limited
3 Queen Square London W.C.1
Second edition, revised, 1960
First published in this edition 1968
Reprinted 1971
Printed in Great Britain by
Latimer Trend & Co Ltd Whitstable
All rights reserved

ISBN 0 571 05502 8 (Faber Paper Covered Edition)
ISBN 0 571 08621 7 (Hard Bound Edition)

FOR
LENOCHKA

# Contents

# *Preface*
## to the First Edition

---

This essay was published in America last year as the first volume of a series devoted to 'The Makers of Modern Literature'. Its point of departure is the recent death of James Joyce. Two years before, with the publication of *Finnegans Wake*, his work in progress was brought to its appointed completion. At the same time he relaxed his lifelong habits of personal reticence to co-operate with his biographer, Herbert Gorman. Through Mr. Gorman's efforts and through other sources, documents have become available to students and collectors in this country, which clarify the different stages of Joyce's development as an artist. Meanwhile, in the wider world, the pace of events has so accelerated that we have already begun to look back upon his work as upon the legacy of an earlier period. This would seem to be the proper occasion for a full critical appraisal. It is not the author but the reader of this book who must make the appraisal. If this book helps to overcome the obstacles that sometimes discourage the reader of Joyce, it will have served its function.

During his lifetime, philistine prejudice and esthetic snobbishness combined to envelop Joyce in controversy. Now that his work is completed, we must try to understand its significance, and to place him—without extenuation or malice—against the broad perspectives of literary history. We must recognize both his striking originality and his deep sense of tradition. The more we study him, the less unique he seems, and the more he seems to have in common with other significant writers of the past and of the present. With writers, there is always what Henry James called 'the figure in the carpet', a pattern woven into the warp of historic necessity by the woof of artistic intention, which it is the task of criticism to discover and to set forth. With Joyce, this figure has been obscured by a luxuriant profusion of language and detail, but it is none the less implicit in everything he wrote. If I have made it unduly explicit, I can only plead that oversimplification has not been the usual complaint of Joyce's readers.

Since this book is designed to be read in close conjunction with Joyce's books, I have used or indicated his own words wherever they seemed most appropriate. They need no apology, though mine may. In attempts to deal with his later prose, as in attempts to explain a poem or a joke, paraphrase sounds particularly flat. To facilitate cross-reference to Joyce's text, the pages of his respective books are denoted by superior numerals. For permission to quote I must now thank the holders of his English copyrights: Jonathan Cape for the passages from *Dubliners*, *Exiles*, and *A Portrait of the Artist as a Young Man*; John Lane for the quotations from *Ulysses*; and Faber & Faber for the material from *Finnegans Wake*. I must also thank Messrs. John Lane The Bodley Head Limited for the privilege of citing material from Herbert Gorman's *James Joyce*. Like all students of Joyce, I am indebted to the zealous commentary of Stuart Gilbert, *James Joyce's 'Ulysses'*, as well as to Mr. Gorman's faithful biography. With these two indispensable books I should include a third—the *Word Index to James Joyce's 'Ulysses'*, compiled by Miles L. Hanley with assistance from the National Youth Administration (U.S.A.). Here, too, I should set down my thanks to Messrs. Allen & Unwin for the use of a paragraph from Synge's preface to his *Playboy of the Western World*.

To the many critics who have written on Joyce, I have tried to record my specific obligations. Beyond these, I should mention my general indebtedness to the studies of Valery Larbaud, Ernst Robert Curtius, S. Foster Damon, and Edmund Wilson. To James Laughlin IV, I owe the original suggestion for this volume, a number of suggestions along the way, and permission to plagiarize freely from my article, 'On First Looking into *Finnegans Wake*', in *New Directions in Prose & Poetry* 1939. I am especially grateful to Theodore Spencer for sharing not only his interest in Joyce, but his opportunity to consult the unpublished manuscript of the *Portrait of the Artist* now in the Harvard College Library. It is a satisfaction to learn that this discarded version is at last to appear in print. To other friends I should like to express my gratitude— to Albert Erskine, Jr., for his editorial advice, to John V. Kelleher for his Irish lore, to John A. Lester, Jr., for his valued assistance, to F. O. Matthiessen for his critical encouragement, to John J. Slocum for photostats of items in his collection, and to Emily Sweetser for help with the index. This edition, apart from the needed bibliographical adjustments, has involved no special revision. The English reader may be struck—I hope not too harshly— by occasional divergences of usage or attitude. But he will know, better than the American writer, where to make allowances for a different angle of observation. Today neither will be inclined to exaggerate the difference.

H.L.

*Eliot House,*
*Cambridge, Mass.*
*3rd October* 1942

# *Preface*
## to the Revised Edition

It is now almost eighteen years since the foregoing paragraphs were printed for the first time. They, in their turn, marked the outcome of a train of thought which had been set in motion two years before, when *Finnegans Wake* was published. As it happened, I was one of the disappointingly small number of reviewers who treated the work at the length and with the respect that it should have been able to take for granted. Though I held some reservations and made some wild guesses and missed Joyce only knew how much, somehow I must have met his mind here and there; for he kindly registered his response in a note which gave Mr. Laughlin the notion of putting me down for the volume on Joyce in his newly projected series, 'The Makers of Modern Literature'. I agreed to that proposal in the happy thought that my subject would be living longer and writing more, and that this summary essay on his life-work would be a distant holiday for a young scholar then professionally immersed in Elizabethan drama.

The occasion came all too soon, amid circumstances of general distraction which—as I see now—have left their imprint upon these pages. Perhaps the book itself, such as it was, such as it remains, might be characterized by the sub-title attached to its last chapter in Spanish translation: *un epitafio*. One does not bring an epitaph up to date, and it is with some reluctance that I have seen my way toward the preparation of this revised edition. Precisely because there has been so much more to say, and because so much of it has been or is being so well said by so many others, I would rather read about Joyce than continue to write about him. Yet the continuance of any interest prompts second thoughts,

13

stimulates palinodes, and provides opportunities to atone for sins of omission. In editing *The Portable James Joyce* (misleadingly entitled *The Essential James Joyce* in England), I emphasized certain minor works which are slighted here, *Exiles* and *Pomes Penyeach*. On the other hand, that plan of selection resulted in slighting Joyce's major works, *Ulysses* and *Finnegans Wake*.

Retrospect brings some degree of detachment; and though I cannot evaluate my effort, I think I can place it. It had the advantage of coming at the moment when the controversy around the living Joyce had just ended. His friends had played their important part as defenders, comforters, and intermediaries. He still had his detractors, but their opinions counted for less and less; too many fellow writers and able critics had rallied to his cause. Judicial enlightenment had removed the ban that had long attempted to keep *Ulysses* from the Anglo-American reading public. Has there ever before been so short a transition between ostracism and canonization? Suddenly, by ceasing to be a contemporary, Joyce had become a classic. Then it was easy enough to recognize his historic role, to trace his literary affiliations, and even to reconcile his iconoclasm with the forces it had revolted against. Those changes in status and interpretation—I suspect—followed a larger sequence of esthetic shifts as the twentieth century was moving from its first to its second generation, and from Bohemia to Academe.

Many of us, who bought our copies of *Ulysses* abroad and smuggled them through the customs, gained a collusive thrill which sometimes returns in the form of nostalgia. But such unearned emotions are checked for me when I remember how a local bookseller was jailed for selling a surreptitious copy, despite the eloquent testimony of F. O. Matthiessen. An immersion in Joyce's writings was one of the most demanding and most rewarding studies of my undergraduate days. None the less, it had to be pursued without credit or guidance. Hence, when I had a chance to teach a course, I managed to persuade my tolerant colleagues that such pursuits were worthy of a place in the curriculum; and when Mr. Laughlin made his hurried request for a manual, I could pass along my pedagogical experience to other students in and outside the university. Today it would be hard to find a college where Joyce is not on some syllabus or other. This is ironic but not improper, given a writer as deeply concerned as he was with the process of education and with the transmission of culture.

Naturally, I share the hope of my publishers that this little book will have an extended usefulness in introducing Joyce to later readers. However, I cannot claim to have done much rewriting. On rereading, I felt that my earlier conceptions had not basically altered; and that if my presentation had any merit, it was that of a tightly knit design which could not helpfully be distended or loosened. Even with regard to *Finnegans Wake*, where there has been so much subsequent elucidation, I have had to make only a few corrections, since my two chapters stressed ideas and techniques, using illustrations selectively. Consequently, there are no more than thirty-odd revisions throughout, in most cases comprising a changed word or two. Since the bibliography was hopelessly obsolete, and since it has been rendered unnecessary by the very plenitude of publications and reprints, it has been discarded altogether. In its stead I have written a longish postscript, 'Revisiting Joyce'. There I have undertaken a running comment on some of the new material, both documentary and critical, which has carried our understanding beyond my original text.

H.L.

*Modern Language Centre,*
*Harvard University*
*21st June* 1959

# I

---

*The Uncreated Conscience*

# 1. Reality

The problem of the artist in the twentieth century was posed a generation ago. 'All art is a collaboration,' wrote John Millington Synge in his preface to *The Playboy of the Western World*, 'and there is little doubt that in the happy ages of literature, striking and beautiful phrases were as ready to the story-teller's or the playwright's hand, as the rich cloaks and dresses of his time. . . . In countries where the imagination of the people, and the language they use, is rich and living, it is possible for a writer to be rich and copious in his words, and at the same time to give the reality, which is the root of all poetry, in a comprehensive and natural form. In the modern literature of towns, however, richness is found only in sonnets, or prose poems, or in one or two elaborate books that are far away from the profound and common interests of life. One has, on one side, Mallarmé and Huysmans producing this literature; and on the other, Ibsen and Zola dealing with the reality of life in joyless and pallid words.'

This was the mutually exclusive choice that writers had found themselves facing, as the nineteenth century waned. The resulting disequilibrium is what makes so much of the literature of the eighteen-nineties, in retrospect, seem trivial or top-heavy. Richness, on one side, petulantly glimmers through the symbolism of Huysmans; reality, on the other, darkly palpitates in the naturalism of Zola. As usual, the most conspicuous models are to be sought in France, and the most divergent extremes are to be found elsewhere. Wilde is one Anglo-Irish example, Shaw another. The first leaves of Stefan George's *Blätter für die Kunst* appeared during the very year in which Gerhart Hauptmann's *Die Weber* took the German theatre by assault. In Italy there was D'Annunzio, and also Verga; in Russia there was Merezhkovsky, as well as Gorky. And in America, the dilemma which perplexed Henry James and Mark Twain has not been resolved by the generation of Cabell and Lewis, or Wilder and Hemingway.

But naturalism and symbolism, like other -isms, can come to terms. Otherwise it would not be possible to comprehend Flaubert, or to reconcile *L'éducation sentimentale* with *La tentation de Saint-Antoine*. In *Madame Bovary*, it might even be suggested, reality and richness are bedfellows: the doctor dreams of domestic comforts and his child, while his wife fancies Italian valleys and a lover. Here, obviously, is an unstable *ménage*. Symbolist and naturalist, during the next generation, are designed to drift apart and to set up opposing cults of art and nature. The scientific pretensions and humanitarian sympathies of the naturalists are most conscientiously embodied in the immense collective novel which Zola sub-titled 'a natural and social history'. The increasingly specialized aims of the symbolists are stated by their most acute critical intelligence, Remy de Gourmont, as 'individualism in literature and freedom in art'. To their slogan of '*l'art pour l'art*' the retort was '*une tranche de vie*'.

If we consider Flaubert—who formulated so many of its issues —the patriarch of modern fiction, we can regard the writers of the *fin de siècle* as a second generation, and our immediate contemporaries as a fourth. It is to the third generation, then, that Synge addressed his manifesto. Ireland, he proposed, was the ideal setting for a glad reunion between reality and richness, a dialectical synthesis of the naturalistic tradition and the symbolistic reaction. In Irish life and language, he indicated, writers would find both a vital theme and an expressive medium. With the Irish literary movement—with the achievement of Synge himself in the drama, of Yeats in poetry, and Joyce in fiction—these indications have been filled out. It would be hard to find a comparable body of writing, without going all the way back to the Elizabethans, in which the qualities of highly imaginative expression and closeness to familiar experience are so profusely intermingled.

Now that the last of these three major figures has been gathered

—with William Butler Yeats—'into the artifice of eternity', it is time to ask how far the Celtic renascence has shone in their reflected lustre. It is true that Edward Martyn and George Moore had imported Ibsen and Zola, and that Arthur Symons had translated the poetry of the *symbolistes* for the benefit of Yeats. Yet the equilibrium between life and beauty was fitfully achieved and precariously sustained. To have great poets, according to Whitman, you must have great audiences. Whether you blame the authors or the spectators, it must be admitted that the Irish audience showed little patience with Yeats and Synge. As for Joyce, his books could not and cannot be published or sold in his native country. They are of Irishmen and by an Irishman, but not for Irishmen; and their exclusion was Joyce's loss as well as Ireland's.

A literary movement has been defined, by one of the epigones of the Celtic renascence, as 'five or six people who live in the same town and hate each other cordially'. When the people are Irishmen and the town is Dublin, the possibilities are fairly electric. Joyce, an authentic Dubliner and a competent hater, might have qualified as a member in good standing of the Irish literary movement, but he chose to remain on the periphery. In birth and background he differed from the Anglo-Irish intellectuals; for him their amateurish zeal took the bloom off the culture they were attempting to revive. They were older, and less curious about the widening horizons of European letters. They had lived in England, and conceived the Irish character as an interesting exhibit for the Abbey Theatre. They had never responded to the Catholic catechism, and were vulnerable to private metaphysics and theosophic visions. They were poets who looked to politics for a renascence in which Pre-Raphaelitism would go hand in hand with Home Rule.

For Joyce, Ireland was too much of a reality to be viewed through the haze of Celtic twilight. His development started from the point they were striving to attain, and went in the direction from which they had come. Irish politics charged the atmosphere he breathed in childhood. The nun *manquée* who took care of him, and whom he described as Mrs. Riordan in *A Portrait of the Artist as a Young Man*, kept two brushes on her dresser—one for Charles Stewart Parnell, and the other for Michael Davitt, the nationalist leader who had gone to jail with Ireland's uncrowned king. The Joyce family boasted a remote connection with Daniel O'Connell, the liberator. The first school to which they sent their son was linked by traditional associations with the memory of the eighteenth-century patriot, Wolfe Tone. Family tradition staunchly maintains that Joyce's first published work was a broadside written at the age of nine, attacking the politician who had risen to power by the fall of Parnell, and bearing the resonant title, *Et Tu, Healy?*

Joyce's relations with the circle of Irish writers that had emerged during his school days are most concisely put in the words with which he is said to have acknowledged an introduction to Yeats: 'You are too old for me to help you.' His own maturity did nothing to modify this brash condescension. In the opening scene of *Ulysses*, Irish art is dismissed as 'the cracked lookingglass of a servant', and the old milkwoman representing Ireland mistakes Gaelic for French. Later, in the library episode, Joyce takes occasion to pay his sardonic respects to the chief personalities of the literary revival. It is hardly surprising that one of these personalities, W. K. Magee, the thoughtful Irish critic who writes under the name of John Eglinton, greeted *Ulysses* as 'a violent interruption of what is known as the Irish literary renascence'. A broader view of the situation, and a closer comprehension of Joyce's undeviating aims, prompted a continental critic, Valery Larbaud, to announce that Ireland had at last made 'a sensational re-entry into high European literature'.

It is not easy to identify Joyce with any movement. His personal objectives cut him off completely from the Irish revolution. Little reviews record the clearest response to his writing, and an imagist anthology includes one of his early poems. But he cannot be included in any school; he was a school by himself. In spite of his skill at languages, he would learn small Gaelic and less Greek. Gaelic was the shibboleth of his nationalistic classmates, and Greek was the mark of the Anglo-Irish caste at Trinity College. Ultimately, he would create his own language. Meanwhile, he sat at the feet of a sterner master than Dr. Hyde or Professor Mahaffy: he studied Norse so that he could read Henrik Ibsen in the original. And when Ibsen's hero shouted, 'I am Norwegian by birth but cosmopolitan in spirit', his young Irish disciple determined to meet him on common ground. He determined, like Ibsen, to be a European man of letters, whose iconoclastic influence would transcend national boundaries, break down parochial prejudices, open windows and slam doors.

Seven cities claimed the author of the *Odyssey*. The author of *Ulysses*—and of *Dubliners* and *Exiles*—lived in as many, each more polyglot and metropolitan than the last. The whole of his creative career, and the greater part of his life, were spent on the continent of Europe. His work is conceived less in the spirit of Irish renascence than of European decadence. It is quite as characteristic of Parisian culture in the Alexandrian period between the first and second world wars, as of Dublin life at the turn of the nineteenth century. *In partibus infidelium*, however, Joyce remained a wild-goose, an Irishman abroad. Expatriation was a gesture of rebellion, but of typically Irish rebellion, against the British garrison and the Roman church. He sought out compatriots; he subscribed to Dublin sporting papers; he translated Yeats and Synge into Italian. Though painfully *déraciné*, his roots had gone so deep that he continued to draw upon reserves of vitality from the soil of Ireland.

Joyce liked to regard strangers, in terms of Chamfort's maxim, as 'contemporary posterity'. To them he addressed his writing, and it won earliest and fullest recognition on the continent and in America. Deliberately he submitted it, bristling with local allusions and topical references and other novelties, to a more rigorous test than most writers expect to undergo within their lifetime. It would be self-deception for us, as strangers, to overlook these obstacles. Necessarily, we approach his work the wrong way. Without pretending to rival his linguistic accomplishments or match his eccentric erudition, those of us who have the curiosity to read him at all can ordinarily limp along after him down bypaths of language and learning. What he also takes for granted, and what we totally lack, is a thorough grounding in Irish life, in the streets and landmarks, the sounds and smells, the pubs and stews of his native city. 'Dear Dirty Dublin', if it means anything to us, is the name of a book by Lady Morgan.

We could not imagine a situation more likely to distort any critical efforts to realize an author's intentions. From this tangent, what should be familiar seems utterly recondite and what should be recondite seems vaguely familiar. We miss the core of humanity at the basis of Joyce's work, and manage—by way of slight compensation—to catch hold of the fragments of his fantasy as they ramify outward. When Joyce's *alter ego* went to school, he wrote on the fly-leaf of his geography:

> *Stephen Dedalus*
> *Class of Elements*
> *Clongowes Wood College*
> *Sallins*
> *County Kildare*
> *Ireland*
> *Europe*
> *The World*
> *The Universe*

This jejune scrawl charts the course of Joyce's writing, although whether you would call it centrifugal or centripetal depends upon your point of view. It resembles one of those time-tables that you read downwards on your way to the country and upwards on your way home. Joyce's development as an artist proceeded from insular reality to cosmopolitan richness, but to follow him you must reverse the direction. That is less difficult than it might seem, for his whole hierarchy is always accessible. If it is breath-taking to be suddenly projected from the suburbs of Dublin to the outer circle of the seven spheres, it is heart-warming to hear the seraphim and cherubim speak with an Irish accent. The Class of Elements and the Universe belong to the same frame of reference, and they function together in a kind of cosmic regionalism.

Joyce is the most self-centred of universal minds. Far more explicitly than most writers, even those who made the most romantic pageants of their exhibitionistic hearts, he exploited his personal experience for purposes of literary documentation. His youth in Dublin, subject to the limitations of poor eyesight, the perceptions of acute hearing, the exaggerations of immaturity, the natural bonds of emotion and unnatural tensions of resistance, furnished his only subject-matter. He forgot nothing and forgave nothing. Any resemblance to actual persons and situations, living or dead, was carefully cultivated. The earliest objection to his writing was that he had mentioned actual streets and well-known taverns of Dublin, and reported innuendoes about King Edward VII. His books are crowded with public characters who appear under their own names, or private characters who turn out to be friends of the author in disguise. Enemies of the author, from time to time, are introduced by name into incongruous situations. Like Dante, Joyce took considerable satisfaction in paying off old scores.

Since Joyce's life is so inextricably woven into his work, we shall be confronted with the details of his biography as soon as we turn to the pages of his books. In approaching them, we need only bear in mind the most external circumstances of their composition. They fit into a geographical pattern, broadly bounded by many cities, the successive stations of a luckless pilgrimage. James Augustine Aloysius Joyce, the eldest child of John Stanislaus Joyce and the former Mary Jane Murray, was born in Dublin on 2nd February 1882, a few months before the Phoenix Park murders registered their violent protest against the Castle régime. By nature he was endowed with a delicate physique, a seemly appearance, and a subtle intelligence; with eyes so weak that long periods of his life were passed in a state of virtual blindness, and a tenor voice so fine that he very nearly became a professional musician.

In school, first in the Class of Elements at Clongowes Wood and then at Belvedere College in Dublin, he received the proverbially indelible training of the Jesuits. His higher studies were pursued in due course, not at the protestant Trinity College, but at University College, the centre of a brief and brilliant Catholic literary tradition. Cardinal Newman, the original rector, had there tried to put into practice his *Idea of a University*, and Father Gerard

Manley Hopkins had for a while been professor of Greek. Joyce is remembered as a keen but intractable student, chiefly interested in subjects like philosophy and modern languages, which nourished his appetite for esthetic theory and contemporary European literature. *A Portrait of the Artist as a Young Man* carries the story of his life up to 1902, when he took his degree and departed for France. In Paris he soon abandoned a notion of studying medicine, and with much deliberation began to prepare himself for a literary career.

When, after a few months, these preparations were interrupted by news of his mother's illness, he returned to Ireland to be present at her death-bed. A hostile witness, Dr. Oliver Gogarty, has described the restless and ribald Joyce of the ensuing period as a kind of modern Goliard, 'a medical student's pal'. Joyce had his revenge when he celebrated his medical companion, in dactylic dimeter, as the Malachi Mulligan of *Ulysses*. During the summer of 1904, while Joyce was teaching in a school near Dublin, the day passed which he was so painstakingly to recapture by means of that work. In the autumn, with Nora Barnacle, who was to become his wife, he left Ireland to make his home on the continent, promising to produce a great book in ten years. This decade was mainly spent in Trieste, where both of his children were born. By his drudgery as a teacher of languages in a Berlitz school, he earned the barest living for his family. He eked out one brief interlude as a bank clerk in Rome.

His best effort, and all his spare time, were devoted to his writing; but he worked slowly, and without encouragement. A small volume of poems, *Chamber Music*, was issued by a London publisher in 1907—Joyce's first book. Hardly anything he ever wrote was published without a struggle. If the editors accepted his manuscripts, the printers refused to set them up; if the publishers brought out his books, the censors destroyed them. If the charge was not obscenity, it was blasphemy; if not blasphemy, it was treason. When his writing was banned in Ireland, it was published in England; when banned in England, it was published in America; and at length it was banned in America. For years after he had become one of the acknowledged masters of English prose, it was illegal to read his books in any English-speaking country. Nor did every potential sponsor let him down so politely as the English printing firm which refused to handle the *Portrait of the Artist* because 'we would not knowingly undertake any work of a doubtful character even though it may be a classic'.

In 1912 Joyce visited Dublin for the last time, in a futile endeavour to bring out his book of stories. When Messrs. Maunsel, who were publishers-in-ordinary to the Irish revival, broke their contract with him and burned the sheets of *Dubliners*, he made up his mind never to return to Ireland. As soon as he reached the continent, he found a way of retaliating. Some years before, when he first went to Italy, he had expressed his revulsion from Dublin in a poem, 'The Holy Office', which depends, for its scatological sarcasm, on a literal interpretation of the Aristotelian doctrine of catharsis. Now, he persuaded an imperturbable Dutch printer to set up another doggerel broadside, 'Gas from a Burner', which he subsequently caused to be circulated among his acquaintances in Dublin. Its embittered gaiety crystallizes, more pointedly than the gossip and recrimination of memoirs, Joyce's attitude toward his country and contemporaries.

> *. . . But I owe a duty to Ireland:*
> *I hold her honour in my hand,*
> *This lovely land that always sent*
> *Her writers and artists to banishment*
> *And in a spirit of Irish fun*
> *Betrayed her own leaders, one by one.*
> *'Twas Irish humour, wet and dry,*
> *Flung quicklime into Parnell's eye . . .*
> *O Ireland my first and only love*
> *Where Christ and Caesar are hand and glove!*
> *O lovely land where the shamrock grows!*
> *(Allow me, ladies, to blow my nose) . . .*
> *I printed folklore from North and South*
> *By Gregory of the Golden Mouth:*
> *I printed poets, sad, silly and solemn:*
> *I printed Patrick What-do-you Colm:*
> *I printed the great John Milicent Synge*

*Who soars above on an angel's wing*
*In the playboy shift that he pinched as swag*
*From Maunsel's manager's travelling-bag . . .*
*And a play on the Word and Holy Paul*
*And some woman's legs that I can't recall*
*Written by Moore, a genuine gent*
*That lives on his property's ten per cent . . .*
*But I draw the line at that bloody fellow,*
*That was over here dressed in Austrian yellow,*
*Spouting Italian by the hour*
*To O'Leary Curtis and John Wyse Power*
*And writing of Dublin, dirty and dear,*
*In a manner no blackamoor printer would bear.*

The tenth year of exile was, as Joyce had prophesied, his *annus mirabilis*. In 1914 *Dubliners* was finally published, the *Portrait of the Artist* completed, *Exiles* composed, and *Ulysses* begun. In 1914 also, the first World War began. Joyce, having pledged neutrality to the Austrian government, was permitted to settle in Zürich, then a sanctuary for expatriates. There, while he was working on *Ulysses*, Lenin was waiting for his sealed train. Joyce, by virtue of his oath and of his eyesight, felt *au-dessus de la mêlée*. Through the intercession of friends in England, he had been granted a small sum from the Privy Purse; now, in the general cause of culture, he attempted to organize a company of English players. The project started successfully with a performance of *The Importance of Being Earnest*, but dwindled into a serio-comic litigation over a pair of trousers which an attaché at the British Consulate had bought, in order to play the role of Algernon Moncrieff with becoming elegance. Joyce was not above this particular battle. He nursed his grudge into the book: the attaché, Carr, becomes the English private who picks a fight with the Irish hero, while the apparition of Edward VII—exorcised from *Dubliners*— hovers above the scene with a bucket labelled *Défense d'uriner*.

After the war Joyce and his family gravitated to Paris. Appropriately, in that capital of the cosmopolitan arts, *Ulysses* was finished, and published on its author's fortieth birthday. Since Ibsen's plays were first produced, it is not easy to think of a literary event which occasioned sharper reactions or wider consequences. Critical success followed *succès de scandale*, and no writer has cared less than Joyce about popular approval. Though shielded from his books, a generation of English and American writers grew up under his influence. From various countries homage came in the almost inconceivable form of foreign translations. Meanwhile, the generosity of an admirer had secured Joyce against financial worries. Living in austere leisure, protected by a small coterie of friends, he undertook a final series of literary experiments. Over a number of years, *Work in Progress* materialized in the international journal, *transition*; in 1939, it took definitive shape as his last book, *Finnegans Wake*. In the following year, with the collapse of the Third Republic, Joyce was forced to leave Paris and return to Zürich. There he died, after an intestinal operation, on 13th January 1941.

When the notorious public controversies, the fabulous literary exploits, and the wild-goose chases of Joyce's career are thus reduced to sober outline, his itinerary is divisible into three parts. The first part covers his experience in Ireland during the first twenty years of his life, and is itself covered by the *Portrait of the Artist*. The middle period comprises the next two decades, devoted to creative activity in Austria and Switzerland, culminating with the appearance of *Ulysses*. His final years in France found their unique expression in *Finnegans Wake*. Each of these three major works—whether they should be called novels is a question we shall not beg at this point—corresponds to one of those three periods. Joyce also left three *opuscula*: a volume of short stories, a drama, a collection of verse. These early and exploratory writings are closely related in composition and theme to the *Portrait of the Artist*, which is itself a distillation of a much broader body of material. They should help to compensate for the comparative slightness of the *Portrait of the Artist*, in contradistinction to the monumental scale and elaborated texture of *Ulysses* and *Finnegans Wake*.

By considering these works in their natural order, we shall be tracing a course which is not peculiar to Joyce, but which other gifted imaginative writers have already taken, and still others may be expected to follow. It is a course which is better described by the archly uncapitalized catchword of Joyce's late colleagues, *transition*, than by the untimely fanfares of a renascence. More spectacularly than any of his contemporaries, Joyce embraces the extremes of richness and reality—not so much the perfect fusion of these elements as their bitter opposition. As we gain perspective, we can see that compromise is not easy and choice is not free. The derivations of naturalism, as a disciplined revision of nineteenth-century realism, are perfectly clear. The prospects of symbolism, as a testing-ground for the literary experiments of our own day, are purely speculative. But today it is too late to be surprised by the reflection that one movement belongs to the past and the other to the future. The history of literature since Flaubert can be charted in these terms, and the recently completed lifework of Joyce will provide the literary historian with his most impressive evidence.

Joyce himself was acutely conscious of his transitional role. When invited to lecture at Trieste on two English writers, he chose the most matter-of-fact and the most visionary, Defoe and Blake. In one of his earliest attempts to take a position, he characterized the poet as 'a mediator between the world of reality and the world of dreams'. The process of mediation, on the whole, has not been as difficult for other times as it is for ours. Joyce's successes, in the face of disheartening odds, evince personal talents of the very highest calibre—talents which might another time have produced a Rabelais or Cervantes, a Milton or Goethe. His very failures are the outcome of that state of cultural disintegration which he so keenly sensed and so comprehensively rendered. No naturalist has ventured a more exhaustive and unsparing depiction of the immediacies of daily life. No symbolist has spun more subtle and complicated cobwebs out of his own tortured entrails. *Ulysses* occupies a pivotal position in Joyce's own development and in the culture of the twentieth century, '*A la fois réaliste et symboliste*', in the phrase of Edmond Jaloux, looking backwards and forwards it stands, an enigmatic and labyrinthine monument.

# Reality

*A Portrait of the Artist as a Young Man* fits squarely into the naturalistic tradition, and *Finnegans Wake* can only be classified as a symbolistic experiment. There are germs of symbolism in the early book, of course, and a residue of naturalism in the recent one. It is paradoxical that the *Portrait of the Artist*, so direct in treatment, should be devoted to the problems of art; while *Finnegans Wake*, where the figure of the artist has disappeared into the complexities of his technique, should be concentrated upon the *minutiae* of city life. We shall not be confused by this paradox if we recognize from the outset that Joyce's most protean variations are played upon two obsessive themes—the city and the artist. The connection between these themes is all the more poignant because it is so slight. It is as tenuous and strained as the connection between life and art in our time. The modern metropolis is lacking in beauty; the contemporary writer is without a community. The city finds its obvious vehicle of expression in naturalism. The artist, left to his own devices, turns in the other direction. *Ulysses* is an attempted synthesis, foredoomed to failure by the very conditions it assumes.

The artist is an exile from the city. He has renounced his ties with friends and family, church and country. In isolation, he seeks to cultivate the traditions and techniques of his craft, to recreate life artificially through the medium of words. But words—means of communication as well as expression—have an independent life which is active and gregarious, which derives its velocity from the lips of men. With each successive work, like carrier pigeons from abroad, they come home to roost in Dublin. It may be that the artist is inspired by a very human feeling of nostalgia. Again, he may be motivated by a superhuman impulse to play God. Having left his religion behind with his community, he may strive—by whatever demiurgy he can command—to call forth an order of his own, to impose a private pattern upon the chaos of his experience. In the days of decadent Rome, a mind like Augustine's could take refuge in the Christian conception of a *City of God*. With the modern intellectual, art has taken the place of religion. He feels the need to create a city of art, a Byzantium.

# 2. The City

---

When *We Dead Awaken*, which Ibsen called his 'dramatic epilogue', was the occasion for Joyce's prologue. In 1900 he made a precocious first appearance in the *Fortnightly Review* with a eulogy of Ibsen's tired final performance. It is possible to understand, if not to feel, the attractions which this parable of art and life held for Joyce. The attempt of an ageing sculptor and his former model to recapture the spirit which had animated his masterpiece, 'The Resurrection', is smothered in a snowstorm; while his young wife and a fourth character, an energetic sportsman, continue up the mountain-side. Forbidding as it sounds, the drama left an impression that Joyce never quite outgrew. In his single play, *Exiles*, the basic situation of a set-to-partners recurs. In his own final work, *Finnegans Wake*, the *motif* of resurrection surges up.

By revising his own account of his early attitudes toward life and art, Joyce has obscured the fact that they stem naïvely out of the naturalist movement. The early version of the *Portrait of the Artist* dwells expansively upon the meeting of minds between the old Norse poet and the perturbed young Celt, 'in a moment of radiant simultaneity'. The most striking of many letters which Herbert Gorman includes in his biography is the English draft, to be rendered into arduous Norwegian, of a salutation addressed by Joyce to Ibsen on his seventy-third birthday in 1901. Although Joyce speaks 'as one of the young generation for whom you have spoken', he seems curiously conscious of his own right to answer for that generation, and to treat Ibsen—as between generations—more as an equal than as a master. 'Do not think me a hero-worshipper—I am not so,' he bluntly informs the old man, and goes on to confide that it was none other than Joyce who first sounded the name of Ibsen in the debating societies at college. The letter, like the rest of Joyce's writing, is a comment on the writer. It is revealing to see what he admires most in Ibsen— 'lofty impersonal power', 'wilful resolution to wrest the secret from life', 'absolute indifference to public canons of art, friends and shibboleths'.

The same year saw another subjective contribution to dramatic criticism from Joyce. His cult of Ibsen had kept him aloof from the Irish Literary Theatre. When he had refused to join the other students in protest against *The Countess Cathleen*, he was not moved by sympathy for Yeats and his colleagues, but by the distrust of the bigoted nationalism which had damned the play. Now, with invidious impartiality, he called for a plague on both houses. The Irish Literary Theatre, he charged, had capitulated to the groundlings, to 'the rabblement of the most belated race in Europe'. The vantage-point of his attack is an intransigent intellectualism, eager to suggest unflattering comparisons between the Irish playwrights and Joyce's cosmopolite allegiances. 'Elsewhere there are men who are worthy to carry on the tradition of the old master who is dying in Christiania. He has already found his successor in the writer of "Michael Kramer", and the third minister will not be wanting when his hour comes.' Since Joyce was at the moment engaged in a translation of that particular play of Hauptmann's, there is perhaps a further inference of apostolic succession to be drawn.

The reception of Synge's *Playboy* and of Sean O'Casey's *The Plough and the Stars* has retroactively justified Joyce's tirade. But at this early stage the sense of grievance, the philistine-baiting, and the exacerbated tone of 'The Day of the Rabblement' seem utterly unprovoked. Misunderstood genius, it would almost seem, is born and not made. The article was bound to be turned down by the college magazine, and Joyce was forced to issue it in an independent pamphlet, with another piece by a revolutionary classmate. In his very first sentence Joyce proclaims the isolation of the artist, by authority of the Italian arch-heretic of Nola, Giordano Bruno, who is cited under a Hibernian *nom de guerre*, 'the Nolan'. Bruno played the same role in Joyce's development that he did in the history of philosophy: he bridged the gap between medieval scholasticism and scientific naturalism. At the moment, his anti-Aristotelian heresies were beckoning Joyce away from Thomistic orthodoxy. In the scattered notes at the end of the *Portrait of the Artist*, which must have been originally jotted down in these days, a conversation with an Italian student is baldly summarized: 'He said Bruno was a terrible heretic. I said he was terribly burned.'[283]

A man who is on the point of leaving the Catholic church is not likely to throw himself heart and soul into the next movement that comes along. It turned out in Joyce's case that, having left the church, he could never bring himself to participate in any other communion—religious, literary, or social. Yet he found it necessary to define his own position at the beginning and to hold it consistently until the end. With a flourish, the nineteen-year-old author of 'The Day of the Rabblement' takes his stand: 'If an artist courts the favour of the multitude he cannot escape the contagion of its fetichism and deliberate self-deception, and if he joins in a popular movement he does so at his own risk. Therefore, the Irish Literary Theatre, by its surrender to trolls, has cut itself adrift from the line of advancement. Until he has freed himself from the mean influences about him—sodden enthusiasm and clever insinuation and every flattering influence of vanity and low ambition—no man is an artist at all.'

These abrupt manifestoes make an *a priori* approach to a literary career. Joyce, however, had come to terms with art before he was willing to practise it. His *juvenilia* are rather critical than creative. His youthful notebooks seem largely devoted to esthetic theories and excerpts from other writers. His essay on James Clarence Mangan, which was sufficiently sophomoric to be accepted by the college magazine, measures that romantic precursor of the Irish revival by the impressionistic standards of Walter Pater's *Renaissance*. A tendency toward abstraction reminds us, again and again, that Joyce came to esthetics by way of theology. He required the sanction of Saint Thomas Aquinas for his art, though not for his belief. In one of the unpublished parts of the *Portrait of the Artist*, he confessed that his thought was scholastic in everything but the premises. He lost his faith, but he kept his categories. There are times, even in his maturest writing, when he still seems to be a realist in the most medieval sense. His treatment of details is copious and concrete, but they seem to be there to fill in an outline, to support a theory, or to illustrate a principle.

The genesis of the writer is usually a familiar story—the story of a sensitive adolescent in an uncongenial environment. As a boy, Joyce took refuge in the romantic richness of books from the drab reality of the streets. The other boys were content to be Paddy Stink and Mickey Mud; he walked alone as Claude Melnotte or the Count of Monte Cristo. Gradually, as he grew and read, Dublin became peopled with phrases and transfigured with associations. He found himself living in his private city, conversing with his favourite authors. There was a place in his city for the Catholic authorities, ancient and modern—but a place among the exciting new dramatists of Europe and the splendid old poets of the Renascence. A walk through Dublin, during his college days, forms a suggestive background for the *Portrait of the Artist*:[199]

The rainladen trees of the avenue evoked in him, as always, memories of the girls and women in the plays of Gerhart Hauptmann; and the memory of their pale sorrows and the fragrance falling from the wet branches mingled in a mood of quiet joy. His morning walk across the city had begun; and he foreknew that as he passed the sloblands of Fairview he would think of the cloistral silverveined prose of Newman; that as he walked along the North Strand Road, glancing idly at the windows of the provision shops, he would recall the dark humour of Guido Cavalcanti and smile; that as he went by Baird's stone cutting works in Talbot Place the spirit of Ibsen would blow through him like a keen wind, a spirit of wayward boyish beauty; and that passing a grimy marine dealer's shop beyond the Liffey he would repeat the song by Ben Jonson which begins;

*I was not wearier where I lay.*

His mind when wearied of its search for the essence of beauty amid the spectral words of Aristotle or Aquinas turned often for its pleasure to the dainty songs of Elizabethans.

When Joyce turns from the speculative to the sensuous, his first results show no further fusion of theory and practice. If his criticism is too abstract, his poetry is too concrete, with an opaque kind of concreteness that may be only another form of abstraction. His plaintive and cloying little stanzas could only have satisfied George Moore's canons of pure poetry. They are not merely empty of meaning—a deficiency which poets have been known to survive—but of colour. The words, almost without visual quality, are conventionally blocked into the metrical patterns. Even the exceptional vividness of 'I hear an army' comes from crying into the night and moaning in sleep, 'clanging' and 'shouting'; the army is heard and not seen. Lyrics in the strictest sense, all of Joyce's poems have the practical virtue that they can be set to music and sung. When they are not about the commonplaces of love, most of them literally treat the subject of music. Yet the title, *Chamber Music*, does not convey the properly descriptive note; *Ulysses* confirms the hint that a scurrilous *double-entendre* was intended. We are constantly reminded that the poet was a musician, but we are also reminded that the musical episode of *Ulysses* takes place in a bar-room.

When Joyce speaks of the daintiness and quaintness of the Elizabethan lyric, he tells us where to look for his own studied frailties. Actually, he comes closer to the tenor vocalizing of Tom Moore than to the polyphony of the madrigalists. He does avoid the self-consciously Irish verbiage of the poets of the revival, though he over-indulges in classical allusion and Shakespearian echo. Such lines as 'Making moan' and 'With many a pretty air' are by no means rare. In the baker's dozen, accumulated over Joyce's middle years, and marketed as *Pomes Penyeach*, the rhythms are rather more fluent and the images more arresting. But Joyce at best is a merely competent poet, moving within an extremely limited range. The poetic medium, narrowly conceived, offers him too little resistance. It offers him a series of *solfeggio* exercises in preparation for his serious work. His real contribution is to bring the fuller resources of poetry to fiction.

The term 'fiction', ever since the novelists of the nineteenth century discovered that truth was stranger, has been misleading. A conscientious pupil of the naturalistic school, Joyce would not invent his material. He would continue to utilize his own experience, though his imagination was to carry him much farther than the naturalists in interpreting and arranging it. The precincts of his observation were restricted, but his perceptions were abnormally acute. He was the sort of person that Henry James advises the novelist to be, 'one of those people on whom nothing is lost'. The friends of his student days were quick to sense that he went among them taking notes. 'So he recorded under Epiphany', says Dr. Gogarty, 'any showing forth of the mind by which he considered one gave oneself away.' Here, from the squirming model for Buck Mulligan, we have a clinical definition of what was to Joyce an essentially mystical concept. The writer, no longer hoping to comprehend modern life in its chaotic fullness, was searching for external clues to its inner meaning.

An epiphany is a spiritual manifestation, more especially the original manifestation of Christ to the Magi. There are such moments in store for all of us, Joyce believed, if we but discern them. Sometimes, amid the most encumbered circumstances, it suddenly happens that the veil is lifted, the burthen of the mystery laid bare, and the ultimate secret of things made manifest. Such a sudden intimation was experienced by Marcel Proust, when he had dipped a bit of *madeleine* into a cup of linden tea. Such a momentary vision, perhaps too intimate to be included in the final version of the *Portrait of the Artist*, had once come to Stephen Dedalus, passing through Eccles Street, before 'one of those brown brick houses which seem the very incarnation of Irish paralysis'. It now seemed to him that the task of the man of letters was to record these delicate and evanescent states of mind, to become a collector of epiphanies. Walking along the beach, in *Ulysses*, he muses upon his own collection, and his youthful resolve to leave copies to all the libraries of the world, including Alexandria.

Such a collection has come down to us by way of *Dubliners*. This doctrine, however, informs all of Joyce's work—the muffled climaxes of the *Portrait of the Artist*, the alcoholic apparitions of

*Ulysses*, and the protracted nightmare of *Finnegans Wake*. Listen for the single word that tells the whole story. Look for the simple gesture that reveals a complex set of relationships. It follows that the writer, like the mystic, must be peculiarly aware of these manifestations. What seem trivial details to others may be portentous symbols to him. In this light, Joyce's later works are artificial reconstructions of a transcendental view of experience. His dizzying shifts between mystification and exhibitionism, between linguistic experiment and pornographic confession, between myth and autobiography, between symbolism and naturalism, are attempts to create a literary substitute for the revelations of religion.

The reader of Joyce is continually reminded of the analogy between the role of the artist and the priestly office. The focal situation of *Dubliners* is that described in 'Araby', where we walk through the streets of the city, glimpsing places 'hostile to romance' through the eyes of a child: 'These noises converged in a single sensation of life for me: I imagined that I bore my chalice safely through a throng of foes.'[31] The same symbol is given a darker purport in the first story of the book, 'The Sisters', when it is recalled that the dying priest had disgraced himself by breaking a chalice. The broken chalice is an emblem, not only of Joyce's interrupted communion, but of the parched life of the metropolitan *Waste Land*. This early story is also glimpsed from the point of view of a small boy. The very first sentence consists entirely of monosyllables, and the paragraph proceeds toward a childish fascination with the word 'paralysis'.

Joyce's intention, he told his publisher, 'was to write a chapter of the moral history of my country and I chose Dublin for the scene because that city seemed to me the centre of paralysis'. In every one of these fifteen case histories, we seem to be reading in the annals of frustration—a boy is disappointed, a priest suffers disgrace, the elopement of 'Eveline' fails to materialize. Things almost happen. The characters are arrested in mid-air; the author deliberately avoids anything like an event. In 'The Boarding House'—when there is some hope of a wedding—the aggressive landlady, the compromised daughter, and the abashed young man are presented in turn, and an actual interview becomes unnecessary. Joyce's slow-motion narrative is timed to his paralysed subject. Both are synchronized with his strangely apocalyptic doctrine, which assigns to both author and characters a passive part. The author merely watches, the characters are merely revealed, and the emphasis is on the technique of exposure.

Realism had already established the artist as an observer; naturalism made him an outsider. In contrast to the promiscuous documentation of earlier novelists, the *tranche de vie* was sliced thin. A writer like Balzac, claiming to be only the secretary of society, could take a rather officious view of his position. The modern writer stands apart, waiting for a chance encounter or a snatch of conversation to give his story away. Strictly speaking, he has no story, but an oblique insight into a broader subject. Things happen just as they always do—the things you read about in the papers. There is business as usual, but it is none of his business. He is not concerned with romantic adventure or dramatic incident. He is concerned with the routines of everyday life, the mechanisms of human behaviour, and he is anxious to discover the most economical way of exposing the most considerable amount of that material.

This is simply an attempt to define what is so often referred to as the *nuance*. The epiphany, in effect, is the same device. Though grounded in theology, it has now become a matter of literary technique. It has become Joyce's contribution to that series of developments which convert narrative into short-story, supplant plot with style, and turn the *raconteur* into a candid-camera expert. The measure of success, in so attenuated a form, is naturally the degree of concentration. The achievements of Chekhov and Katherine Mansfield, or Hemingway and Katherine Anne Porter, can almost be computed in terms of specific gravity. And Joyce, with 'Two Gallants', can say as much in fifteen pages as James T. Farrell has been able to tell us in volume after volume. It is hard to appreciate the originality of Joyce's technique, twenty-five years after the appearance of *Dubliners*, because it has been standardized into an industry. This industry is particularly well equipped to deal with the incongruities and derelictions of metropolitan life. Its typical products are the shrewd Parisian waifs of *Les hommes de bonne volonté* and the well-meaning nonentities who blunder through the pen and pencil sketches of *The New Yorker*.

In their own way, the tangential sketches of *Dubliners* came as close to Joyce's theme—the estrangement of the artist from the city—as does the systematic cross-section of *Ulysses*. They look more sympathetically into the estranged lives of others. They discriminate subtly between original sin and needless cruelty. 'Counterparts', in its concatenation of petty miseries, suggests the restrained pathos of Chekhov's 'Enemies': it begins with an employer rebuking a clerk, and ends—after several drunken rounds—with the clerk beating his little son. Joyce's point of view, like Dickens's, is most intimately associated with the children of his stories. He arranged his book under four aspects—childhood, adolescence, maturity, and public life. As the stories detach themselves, they assume what Joyce called 'a style of scrupulous meanness'. But 'the special odour of corruption', in which he took pride, was by no means peculiar to Dublin. It was also endemic in middle-western villages like Sherwood Anderson's *Winesburg, Ohio*. It was perceived by an expatriate American poet, T. S. Eliot, as he watched the lost souls crowding over London Bridge:

> *Falling towers*
> *Jerusalem Athens Alexandria*
> *Vienna London*
> *Unreal.*

If the vices of Dublin are those of any modern city, the virtues of 'the seventh city of Christendom' are unique. An unconscionable amount of talking and singing and drinking goes on in *Dubliners*. This promotes style and poetry and fantasy—all peculiarly Irish qualities, and talents of Joyce. 'The imagination of the people, and the language they use, is rich and living,' Synge was discovering. The richness of Irish conversation mitigates the sordid realities of Joyce's book. He was always ready to take full advantage of the common speech of his fellow townsmen—the most expressive English he could have encountered anywhere. He could always portray life most vividly when he was writing by ear. What seems an aimless political discussion, in 'Ivy Day in the Committee Room', is really tight dramatic exposition. In the end the dead figure of Parnell dominates the campaign headquarters. It is his birthday, and an amateur poet is persuaded to recite a maudlin and mediocre eulogy. The finishing touch is the comment of the hostile Conservative, when pressed for his opinion: 'Mr. Crofton said that it was a very fine piece of writing.'[152]

Notice the irony, so frequent with Swift, in the use of indirect discourse. In Joyce's attitude, however, there is an underlying ambiguity: he eats his cake and has it. We, too, are moved by the poem, in spite of—or perhaps because of—its cheapness. We are asked to share both the emotion and the revulsion. In 'Clay', with a different situation, we are subjected to the same treatment. The epiphany is no more than the moment when an old laundress stands up and sings 'I dreamt that I dwelt in marble halls'. She is made to boast of wealth, rank, beauty, and love—none of which she has ever possessed—'in a tiny quavering voice'. A listener, affected by this pathetic incongruity, explains his tears by remarking that there is 'no music for him like poor old Balfe'.[118] Here, as so often in Joyce, the music is doing duty for the feeling. The feeling is deliberately couched in a cheap phrase or a sentimental song, so that we experience a critical reaction, and finally a sense of intellectual detachment. Emotionally sated, we shy away from emotion.

Such passages have the striking and uncertain effect of romantic irony. Jean Paul's formula—'hot baths of sentiment followed by cold showers of irony'—still describes them. They show Joyce, in his isolation from society, confronted by the usual romantic dichotomy between the emotional and the intellectual. At his hands, the problem becomes a characteristically verbal one, which allows him to dwell upon the contrast between the rich connotations and the disillusioning denotations of words. Since the days of *Don Quixote* this has been a major premise for fiction. The point of 'Araby' is the glamour of the name, and the undeception of the small boy when he learns that it stands for a prosaic church bazaar. Yet no disillusionment would seem cruel enough to justify the last sentence, which should be contrasted with the objective description of Mr. Crofton's comment: 'Gazing up into the darkness I saw myself as a creature driven and derided by vanity; and my eyes burned with anguish and anger.'[36]

Another point is scored by the same method in 'Grace', where the distance measured lies between the benign effulgence of religious doctrine and the hangover which brings a group of business men back to church. The distinction between words and things, in 'Ivy Day in the Committee Room' and in 'Grace', is ground for political and religious satire. Church and state should enrich the lives of the citizens and impose a pattern on the city, but for Joyce they are tarnished symbols, broken chalices. Meanwhile, the Dubliners go their own ways. Martin Cunningham, the prominent layman, goes to church in 'Grace' and appears at the funeral in *Ulysses*. Bartell D' Arcy, the tenor, sings a few hoarse notes in 'The Dead' and figures in Mrs. Bloom's reminiscences. Mr. O'Madden Burke goes on writing for his paper, and Lenehan goes from bar to bar and book to book.

Joyce puts himself into his early book, not directly this time, but as he might have been if he had remained a Dubliner. Mr. Duffy, the timid socialist clerk in 'A Painful Case', is translating *Michael Kramer*. He meets a lady whose husband does not understand her, and who for some reason bears the name of Joyce's Italian music-master, Sinico. Though he considers falling in love with her, he continues to brood on 'the soul's incurable loneliness'. One day he reads in the newspaper that she has been killed in an accident of her own seeking—again the title is an echo. Again, in *Ulysses*, we hear of her funeral. Death is one of the few things that happen in *Dubliners*; it is the subject of the first and last stories in the volume. The last and longest story, 'The Dead', concerns the brother of a priest we meet in *Ulysses*. Gabriel Conroy is a Stephen Dedalus who stayed on to teach school and write occasional reviews, and who is already beginning to show symptoms of middle age. He is a pompous master of ceremonies at the Christmas party of his musical maiden aunts—incidentally Joyce's, and godmothers of

Stephen Dedalus. Among others, he meets there a girl he knew, a Gaelic student who earnestly upbraids him for having taken his holidays abroad.

But he is a less significant character than his wife, Gretta, and she is not so significant as a memory awakened in her by a snatch of song at the end of the evening. It is the memory of a boy named Michael Furey, who had once loved her and who had died. Gabriel, who had not known of him before, feels a pang of the soul's incurable loneliness. He can never participate in this buried experience, even though it has become a part of the person he has known most intimately; he suddenly recognizes that he and Gretta are strangers. And, as he tries to imagine the dead boy, he realizes that his own identity is no more palpable to others than Michael Furey's is to him. In the light of this epiphany, the solid world seems to dissolve and dwindle, until nothing is left except the relics of the dead and the hosts of the dying. 'One by one, they were all becoming shades.' The final paragraph, in slow, spectral sentences, cadenced with alliteration and repetition, takes a receding view of the book itself. It sets up, like most departures, a disturbing tension between the warm and familiar and the cold and remote. In one direction lies the Class of Elements at Clongowes Wood, in the other the Universe:[255]

A few light taps upon the pane made him turn to the window. It had begun to snow again. He watched sleepily the flakes silver and dark, falling obliquely against the lamplight. The time had come for him to set out on his journey westward. Yes, the newspapers were right: snow was general all over Ireland. It was falling on every part of the dark central plain, on the treeless hills, falling softly upon the Bog of Allen and, farther westward, softly falling into the dark mutinous Shannon waves. It was falling, too, upon every part of the lonely churchyard on the hill where Michael Furey lay buried. It lay thickly drifted on the crooked crosses and headstones on the spears of the little gate, on the barren thorns. His soul swooned slowly as he heard the snow falling faintly through the universe and faintly falling, like the descent of their last end, upon all the living and the dead.

'The Dead' connects *Dubliners* with *Exiles*, and *Exiles*, in turn, is connected with the *Portrait of the Artist*. Joyce was no more a

dramatist than a poet; but *Exiles*, like *Chamber Music*, gave him
another technique to widen the range of fiction. In the light of his
later experiments, his poetry—to our passing glance—has seemed
incurious and conventional. The limitations of his drama are those
of a literal-minded subservience to another convention, to the
school of Ibsen and the naturalists. But Joyce's naturalism goes
far beyond the requirements of the theatre. He not only lays down
stage-directions for green plush furniture and lace curtains; he
even prescribes the sort of planking for the floor of his box-set.
The framework of naturalistic drama, however, gives way to the
personal preoccupations of the artist. *Exiles* ends in the stalemate
between a problem play and a spiritual autobiography.

The problem play is an attempt to externalize the situation of
domestic estrangement in 'The Dead'. Unlike Gabriel Conroy,
Richard Rowan has succeeded in breaking away from Ireland,
making his home in Italy, and becoming a professional writer.
With Bertha—who has accompanied him—and their child, he has
come home to the unforgiving death-bed of his bigoted mother.
He renews old acquaintance with Beatrice Justice, a music teacher
who was his early inspiration, and Robert Hand, a journalist who
was the companion of his student days. The latter, whose easy-
going sensualism is a foil to Richard's tense intellectuality, has an
assignation with Bertha. There is the possibility of a recurrence
of the *renversement des alliances* that occurs in *When We Dead
Awaken*, but it remains a possibility. When Bertha returns to
Richard, protesting her fidelity, he dismisses the issue. 'I will
never know,' he says flatly. Yet it was he who insisted all along,
'You must know me as I am'.

The result of this double enigma is to make Bertha an uncon-
vincing character, much less convincing than the shadowy Gretta
Conroy. For Gretta is seen through a mist of psychological uncer-
tainties; Bertha must face the three-dimensional scrutiny of the
footlights. Joyce's characterization is far too subjective to be
dramatic. In identifying himself with Richard, he cuts himself off
from his other characters. He admits his own failure to penetrate
the lives of others, yet he goes on expecting them to penetrate his.

He questions the very bases of human intercourse, yet his constant effort is to communicate. The mere attempt to write a play upon such a Proustian theme is self-contradictory. No playwright can afford to be a solipsist. Mr. Gorman reveals the significant fact that Joyce had written another play, which he had loftily dedicated to his own soul. Since he destroyed it, we can only conjecture that the title, *A Brilliant Career*, was another of Joyce's romantic ironies.

The place of *Exiles* is unavoidably Dublin, and the time is 'Summer of the year 1912'—the last of the few occasions on which Joyce interrupted his own exile to visit his native city. 'If Ireland is to become a new Ireland she must first become European,' Robert has said, in extenuation of his old friend. Now he engages in a last effort to find a position for Richard in the intellectual life of the city, a professorship of languages at the college. In a quotation from Robert's article, Joyce makes a journalistic attempt to look at 'that bloody fellow That was over here dressed in Austrian yellow'. It trails off in an echo,—*ubi saeva indignatio cor ulterius lacerare nequit*—the epitaph of the melancholy English writer who spent so many embittered years of exile in Dublin, Swift:[134]

Not the least vital of the problems which confront our country is the problem of her attitude towards those of her children who, having left her in her hour of need, have been called back to her now on the eve of her longawaited victory, to her whom in loneliness and exile they have at last learned to love. In exile, we have said, but here we must distinguish. There is an economic and there is a spiritual exile. There are those who left her to seek the bread by which men live and there are others, nay, her most favoured children, who left her to seek in other lands that food of the spirit by which a nation of human beings is sustained in life. Those who recall the intellectual life of Dublin of a decade since will have many memories of Mr Rowan. Something of that fierce indignation which lacerated the heart. . . .

But the homecoming was to take place only in Joyce's imagination. He himself drew the absolute issue between Europe and Ireland, in the days when he first sounded the name of Ibsen and sneered at the theatre of Lady Gregory. He was prepared to stand by that choice intransigently, even if it meant no compromise between art and life. Art he approached speculatively, in terms of critical theories or opaque lyrics. Life he shyly glimpsed, through a series of personal insights into the estrangements of others. His early efforts to find an audience, to end his isolation, finally confirmed him in his sense of the soul's incurable loneliness. Out of his decade of exile, *Chamber Music*, *Dubliners*, and *Exiles* were merely the offshoots of a larger work. *A Portrait of the Artist as a Young Man* was to fulfil the promise that Joyce had made when he left Dublin, and to vindicate the artist to the city.

# 3. The Artist

The history of the realistic novel shows that fiction tends toward autobiography. The increasing demands for social and psychological detail that are made upon the novelist can only be satisfied out of his own experience. The forces which make him an outsider focus his observation upon himself. He becomes his own hero, and begins to crowd his other characters into the background. The background takes on a new importance for its influence on his own character. The theme of his novel is the formation of character; its habitual pattern is that of apprenticeship or education; and it falls into that category which has been distinguished, by German criticism at least, as the *Bildungsroman*. The novel of development, when it confines itself to the professional sphere of the novelist, becomes a novel of the artist, a *Künstlerroman*. Goethe's *Wilhelm Meister*, Stendhal's *Vie d'Henri Brulard*, and Butler's *Way of All Flesh* amply suggest the potentialities of the form.

The *Künstlerroman* offered a tentative solution to the dilemma of Joyce's generation, by enabling writers to apply the methods of realism to the subject of art. It enabled Marcel Proust to communicate experience more fully and subtly than had been done before, because it was his own experience that he was communicating, and because he was an artist to his finger-tips. *A la recherche du temps perdu* has been described as a novel that was written to explain why it was written. But, having come to be written, it offers other novelists little stimulus toward self-portraiture. It is singularly fitting that *Ulysses* should have appeared in the year of Proust's death. The perverse logic of André Gide can still present, in his *Journal des faux-monnayeurs*, the diary of a novelist who is

47

writing a novel about a novelist who is keeping a diary about the novel he is writing. Of course, the *Künstlerroman* has no logical limit; but, like the label on the box of Quaker Oats, it has a vanishing-point. Already it is beginning to look as old-fashioned as Murger's *Vie de Bohême*.

The *Künstlerroman*, though it reverses the more normal procedure of applying the methods of art to the subject of reality, is the only conception of the novel that is specialized enough to include *A Portrait of the Artist as a Young Man*. In 1913, the year before Joyce finished his book, D. H. Lawrence had published his own portrait of the artist, *Sons and Lovers*. Both books convey the claustral sense of a young intelligence swaddled in convention and constricted by poverty, and the intensity of its first responses to esthetic experience and life at large. The extent to which Lawrence warms to his theme is the measure of Joyce's reserve. Characteristically, they may be reacting from the very different institutions behind them—evangelical English protestantism and Irish Catholic orthodoxy—when Lawrence dwells on the attractions of life, and Joyce on its repulsions. The respective mothers of the two artists play a similar role, yet May Dedalus is a wraith beside the full-bodied realization of Mrs. Morel. The characters in *Sons and Lovers* seem to enjoy an independent existence; in the *Portrait of the Artist* they figure mainly in the hero's reveries and resentments. Joyce's treatment of childhood is unrelieved in its sadness: endless generations of choirs of children sounded, for Stephen Dedalus, the same note of pain and weariness that Newman had heard in Vergil. 'All seemed weary of life even before entering upon it.'[186]

The attitude of the novelist toward his subject is one of the critical questions considered by Joyce's subject. Stephen expounds his own esthetic theory, which he designates as 'applied Aquinas', during a walk in the rain with his irreverent friend, Lynch. *Solvitur ambulando*. It should be noted that the principal action of the *Portrait of the Artist*, whether in conversation or reverie, is walking. The lingering images of *Dubliners* are those of people—often children—in the streets. And it was reserved for Joyce to turn the wanderings of Ulysses into a peripatetic pilgrimage through Dublin. He was, in that respect, a good Aristotelian. But he added a personal touch to the critical theory of Aristotle and Aquinas, when he based the distinction between the various literary forms on the relation of the artist to his material. In the lyric, it is immediate; in the epic, the artist presents his material 'in mediate relation to himself and others'; in drama, it is presented in immediate relation to others.[244]

The lyrical form is in fact the simplest verbal vesture of an instant of emotion, a rhythmical cry such as ages ago cheered on the man who pulled at the oar or dragged stones up a slope. He who utters it is more conscious of the instant of emotion than of himself as feeling emotion. The simplest epical form is seen emerging out of lyrical literature when the artist prolongs and broods upon himself as the centre of an epical event and this form progresses till the centre of emotional gravity is equidistant from the artist himself and from others. The narrative is no longer purely personal. The personality of the artist passes into the narration itself, flowing round and round the persons and the action like a vital sea. This progress you will see easily in that old English ballad *Turpin Hero*, which begins in the first person and ends in the third person. The dramatic form is reached when the vitality which has flowed and eddied round each person fills every person with such vital force that he or she assumes a proper and intangible esthetic life. The personality of the artist, at first a cry or a cadence or a mood and then a fluid and lambent narrative, finally refines itself out of existence, impersonalizes itself, so to speak. The esthetic image in the dramatic form is life purified in and reprojected from the human imagination. The mystery of esthetic like that of material creation is accomplished. The artist, like the God of the creation, remains within or behind or beyond or above his handiwork, invisible, refined out of existence, indifferent, paring his fingernails.

This progress you will see easily in the succession of Joyce's works. The cry becomes a cadence in *Chamber Music*; the mood becomes a *nuance* in *Dubliners*. If *Exiles* is unsuccessful, it is because the epiphany is not manifest to others; the artist has failed to objectify the relations of his characters with each other or with the audience. The narrative of the *Portrait of the Artist* has scarcely emerged from the lyrical stage. Whereas *Dubliners* began in the first person and ended in the third, the *Portrait of the Artist* takes us back from an impersonal opening to the notes of the author at the end. The personality of the artist, prolonging and brooding upon itself, has not yet passed into the narration. The shift from the personal to the epic will come with *Ulysses*, and the centre of emotional gravity will be equidistant from the artist himself and from others. And with *Finnegans Wake*, the artist will have retired within or behind, above or beyond his handiwork, refined out of existence.

Except for the thin incognito of its characters, the *Portrait of the Artist* is based on a literal transcript of the first twenty years of Joyce's life. If anything, it is more candid than other autobiographies. It is distinguished from them by its emphasis on the emotional and intellectual adventures of its protagonist. If we can trust the dates at the end of the book, Joyce started to write in Dublin during 1904, and continued to rewrite until 1914 in Trieste. There is reason to believe that he had accumulated almost a thousand pages—and brought Stephen to the point of departure for Paris—when the idea of *Ulysses* struck him, and he decided to reserve those further adventures for the sequel. His provisional title, *Stephen Hero*, with its echo of the ballad of Dick Turpin, marks the book as an early point in his stages of artistic impersonality. As the hero of a pedagogical novel, Stephen is significantly baptized. Saint Stephen Protomartyr was patron of the green on which University College was located, and therefore of the magazine with which Joyce had had his earliest literary misadventures.

Stephen is ever susceptible to the magic of names—particularly of his own last name. Names and words, copybook phrases and schoolboy slang, echoes and jingles, speeches and sermons float through his mind and enrich the restricted realism of the context. His own name is the wedge by which symbolism enters the book. One day he penetrates its secret. Brooding on the prefect of studies who made him repeat the unfamiliar syllables of 'Dedalus', he tells himself that it is a better name than Dolan. He hears it shouted across the surf by some friends in swimming, and the strangeness of the sound is for him a prophecy: 'Now, at the name of the fabulous artificer, he seemed to hear the noise of dim waves and to see a winged form flying above the waves and slowly climbing the air. What did it mean? Was it a quaint device opening a page of some medieval book of prophecies and symbols, a hawklike man flying sunward above the sea, a prophecy of the end he had been born to serve and had been following through the mists of childhood and boyhood, a symbol of the artist forging anew in his workshop out of the sluggish matter of the earth a new soaring impalpable imperishable being?'[192]

The *Portrait of the Artist*, as we have it, is the result of an extended process of revision and refinement. The original version —if an *Ur-Portrait* can be remotely discerned—must have been securely founded upon the bed-rock of naturalistic narrative. It must have been a human document, virtually a diary, to which Joyce confided his notions and reactions not very long after they occurred. In turning from a reproductive to a selective method, he has foreshortened his work. A fragmentary manuscript now in the Harvard College Library touches only the period covered by the last chapter of the printed book, and yet it is nearly as long as the book itself. What is obliquely implied in the final version is explicitly stated in this early draft. The economic situation, for example, as the Dedalus household declines from the genteel to the shabby, is attested by a series of moving vans. In the book there is just one such episode, when Stephen arrives home to hear from his brothers and sisters that the family is looking for another house. Even then the news is not put in plain English, but in evasive pig-Latin.[186] And the book leaves us with only the vaguest impression of the brothers and sisters; Stephen himself is not sure how many there are.

With revision, the other characters seem to have retreated into the background. Stephen's mother, because of the tension between her love and his disbelief, should be the most poignant figure in the book, just as her memory is the most unforgettable thing in *Ulysses*. But the actual conflict is not dramatized; it is coldly analysed by Stephen in the course of one of his interminable walks and talks—this time with the serious-minded Cranly. In the manuscript it gives rise to a powerful scene, on the death of Stephen's sister, when his mother's orthodox piety is humbled before the mysteries of the body. The heroine of the book has been refined out of existence; she survives only in veiled allusions and the initials E—— C——. Emma Clery, in the manuscript, is an enthusiastic young lady with whom Stephen attends a Gaelic class. Their prolonged and pallid romance comes to an unexpected climax when he sees her mackintosh flashing across the green, and abruptly leaves his lesson to confront her with the proposal that they spend the night together and say farewell in the morning. Her reaction explains the interview so cryptically reported in the book, when Stephen turns on the 'spiritual-heroic refrigerating apparatus, invented and patented in all countries by Dante Alighieri'.[287]

The esthetic theory plays a more active part in the earlier version. Instead of being dogmatically expounded to Lynch, it is sounded in the debating society, where it occasions a bitter argument. As Joyce rewrote his book he seems to have transferred the scene of action from the social to the psychological sphere. As he recollected his 'conflicts with orthodoxy' in the comparative tranquillity of exile, he came to the conclusion that the actual struggles had taken place within the mind of Stephen. Discussions gave way to meditations, and scenes were replaced by *tableaux*. Evasion and indirection were ingrained in Joyce's narrative technique. The final effect is that which Shakespearian actors achieve by cutting out all the scenes in *Hamlet* where the hero does not appear. The continuity of dynastic feuds and international issues is obscured by the morbid atmosphere of introspection. Drama has retired before soliloquy.

The Stephen we finally meet is more sharply differentiated from his environment than the figure Joyce set out to describe. How can he be a poet—the other boys have asked him—and not wear long hair? The richness of his inner experience is continually played off against the grim reality of his external surroundings. He is trying 'to build a breakwater of order and elegance against the sordid tide of life without him'.[111] He is marked by the aureole of the romantic hero, like Thomas Mann's outsiders, pressing their noses against the window-panes of a bourgeois society from which they feel excluded. 'To merge his life in the common tide of other lives was harder for him than any fasting or prayer, and it was his constant failure to do this to his own satisfaction which caused in his soul at last a sensation of spiritual dryness together with a growth of doubts and scruples.'[172] At school he takes an equivocal position, 'a free boy, a leader afraid of his own authority, proud and sensitive and suspicious, battling against the squalor of his life and against the riot of his mind'.[103] At home he feels 'his own futile isolation'. He feels that he is scarcely of the same blood as his mother and brother and sister, but stands to them 'rather in the mystical kinship of fosterage, foster child and foster brother'.[112]

Joyce's prose is the register of this intellectual and emotional cleavage. It preserves the contrast between his rather lush verse and his rather dry criticism, between the pathetic children and the ironic politicians of *Dubliners*. All his sensibility is reserved for himself; his attitude toward others is consistently caustic. The claims to objectivity of a subjective novel, however, must be based on its rendering of intimate experience. If Joyce's treatment of Stephen is true to himself, we have no right to interpose any other criteria. Mr. Eliot has made the plausible suggestion that Joyce's two masters in prose were Newman and Pater. Their alternating influence would account for the oscillations of style in the *Portrait of the Artist*. The sustaining tone, which it adopts toward the outside world, is that of precise and mordant description. Interpolated, at strategic points in Stephen's development, are a number of purple passages that have faded considerably.

Joyce's own contribution to English prose is to provide a more fluid medium for refracting sensations and impressions through the author's mind—to facilitate the transition from photographic realism to esthetic impressionism. In the introductory pages of the *Portrait of the Artist*, the reader is faced with nothing less than the primary impact of life itself, a presentational continuum of the tastes and smells and sights and sounds of earliest infancy. Emotion is integrated, from first to last, by words. Feelings, as they filter through Stephen's sensory apparatus, become associated with phrases. His conditioned reflexes are literary. In one of the later dialogues of the book, he is comparing his theory to a trimmed lamp. The dean of studies, taking up the metaphor, mentions the lamp of Epictetus, and Stephen's reply is a further allusion to the stoic doctrine that the soul is like a bucketful of water. In his mind this far-fetched chain of literary associations becomes attached to the sense impressions of the moment: 'A smell of molten tallow came up from the dean's candle butts and fused itself in Stephen's consciousness with the jingle of the words, bucket and lamp and lamp and bucket.'[213]

This is the state of mind that confers upon language a magical potency. It exalts the habit of verbal association into a principle for the arrangement of experience. You gain power over a thing by naming it; you become master of a situation by putting it into words. It is psychological need, and not hyperfastidious taste, that goads the writer on to search for the *mot juste*, to loot the thesaurus. Stephen, in the more explicit manuscript, finds a treasure-house in Skeat's *Etymological Dictionary*. The crucial moment of the book, which leads to the revelation of his name and calling, is a moment he tries to make his own by drawing forth a phrase of his treasure:[189]

—A day of dappled seaborne clouds.—
The phrase and the day and the scene harmonised in a chord. Words. Was it their colours? He allowed them to glow and fade, hue after hue: sunrise gold, the russet and green of apple orchards, azure of waves, the grey-fringed fleece of clouds. No, it was not their colours: it was the poise and balance of the period itself. Did he then love the rhythmic rise and fall of words better than their associations of legend and colour? Or was it that, being as weak of sight as he was shy of mind, he drew less pleasure from the reflection of the glowing sensible world through the prism of a language many coloured and richly storied than from the contemplation of an inner world of individual emotions mirrored perfectly in a lucid supple periodic prose.

The strength and weakness of his style, by Joyce's own diagnosis, are those of his mind and body. A few pages later he offers a cogent illustration, when Stephen dips self-consciously into his word-hoard for suitable epithets to describe a girl who is wading along the beach. We are given a paragraph of word-painting which is not easy to visualize. 'Her bosom was as a bird's, soft and slight, slight and soft as the breast of some dark-plumaged dove,' it concludes. 'But her long fair hair was girlish: and girlish, and touched with the wonder of mortal beauty, her face.'[195] This is incantation, and not description. Joyce is thinking in rhythms rather than metaphors. Specification of the bird appeals to the sense of touch rather than to the sense of sight. What is said about the hair and face is intended to produce an effect without presenting a picture. The most striking effects in Joyce's imagery are those of coldness, whiteness, and dampness, like the bodies of the bathers who shout Stephen's name.

The most vital element in Joyce's writing, in the *Portrait of the Artist* as in *Dubliners*, is his use of conversation. As a reporter of Irish life, for all his reservations, Joyce is a faithful and appreciative listener. It is a tribute to Stephen's ear that, in spite of the antagonism between father and son, Simon Dedalus is such a ripe and congenial character. Like Sean O'Casey's *Paycock*, with all his amiable failings, he is Ireland itself. Though he takes pride in showing Cork to Stephen, and in showing off his son to his own native city, he is really the embodiment of Dublin: 'A medical student, an oarsman, a tenor, an amateur actor, a shouting politician, a small landlord, a small investor, a drinker, a good fellow, a storyteller, somebody's secretary, something in a distillery, a taxgatherer, a bankrupt and at present a praiser of his own past.'[274] The improvident worldliness of John Stanislaus Joyce had made him, in the unforgiving eyes of his son, a foster-parent. So young Charles Dickens, hastening from the blacking-factory to the Marshalsea, came to look upon his father as a horrible example of good-fellowship, a Mr. Micawber.

This disorder, 'the misrule and confusion of his father's house',[185] comes to stand in Stephen's mind for the plight of Ireland. Like Synge's *Playboy*, he must go through the motions of parricide to make good his revolt. Religion and politics, to his adult perception, are among the intimations of early childhood: harsh words and bitter arguments that spoil the taste of the Christmas turkey. Again, as in 'Ivy Day in the Committee Room', or in Lennox

Robinson's *Lost Leader* on the stage, it is the ghost of Parnell that turns conversation into drama. 'Dante', the devout Mrs. Riordan, is true to the Catholic Church in denouncing the disgraced nationalist leader. Mr. Casey, the guest of honour, is of the anti-clerical faction. Mr. Dedalus is by no means a neutral, and some of his mellowest profanity is enlisted in the cause of his dead hero. Mrs. Dedalus softly rebukes him:[38]

—Really, Simon, you should not speak that way before Stephen. It's not right.

—O, he'll remember all this when he grows up, said Dante hotly—the language he heard against God and religion and priests in his own home.

—Let him remember too, cried Mr Casey to her from across the table, the language with which the priests and the priests' pawns broke Parnell's heart and hounded him into his grave. Let him remember that too when he grows up.

The *Portrait of the Artist*, as Joyce's remembrance finally shaped it, is a volume of three hundred pages, symmetrically constructed around three undramatic climaxes, intimate crises of Stephen's youth. The first hundred pages, in two chapters, trace the awakening of religious doubts and sexual instincts, leading up to Stephen's carnal sin at the age of sixteen. The central portion, in two more chapters, continues the cycle of sin and repentance to the moment of Stephen's private apocalypse. The external setting for the education of the artist is, in the first chapter, Clongowes Wood College; in the second, third, and fourth, Belvedere College, Dublin. The fifth and final chapter, which is twice as long as the others, develops the theories and projects of Stephen's student days in University College, and brings him to the verge of exile. As the book advances, it becomes less sensitive to outside impressions, and more intent upon speculations of its own. Friends figure mainly as interlocutors to draw Stephen out upon various themes. Each epiphany—awakening of the body, literary vocation, farewell to Ireland—leaves him lonelier than the last.

A trivial episode at Clongowes Wood seems fraught for Joyce with a profoundly personal meaning. Young Stephen has been unable to get his lessons, because his glasses were broken on the playing-field. Father Dolan, the prefect of studies, is unwilling to accept this excuse, and disciplines Stephen with the boys who have shirked their books. Smarting with pain and a sense of palpable injustice, Stephen finally carries his case to the rector, who shows a humane understanding of the situation. Many years later Father Conmee, the rector, takes a walk through a chapter of *Ulysses*; and Father Dolan—who was actually a Father Daly— pops up with his 'pandybat' in Stephen's nightmare. This schoolboy incident lays down a pattern for Joyce's later behaviour. When he cabled Lloyd George, who had other things on his mind during the first World War, *re* a pair of trousers and *The Importance of Being Earnest*, he was behaving like an aggrieved schoolboy unjustly pandied.

The physical handicap, the public humiliation, the brooding sensibility, the sense of grievance, the contempt for convention, the desire for self-justification, and the appeal to higher authority —these are all elements of Joyce's attitude toward society and toward himself. He had begun his education by questioning the Jesuit discipline; he would finish by repudiating the Catholic faith. Having responded to the urgent prompting of his senses, he would be treated as a sinner; he would refer the ensuing conflict, over the head of religious authority, to the new light of his scientific and naturalistic studies; he would seek, in the end, to create his own authority by the light of his senses. In turning away from Ireland toward the world at large, he would appeal from the parochial Daly to the enlightened Conmee. That miserable day at Clongowes Wood, like that long evening at Combray when M. Swann's visit kept Marcel's mother downstairs, had unforeseen consequences.

Adolescence complicates the second chapter. Stephen is beginning to appreciate beauty, but as something illicit and mysterious, something apart from the common walks of life. Literature has begun to colour his experience, and to stimulate his mind and his senses. His untimely enthusiasm for Lord Byron—'a heretic and immoral too'[92]—provokes a beating at the hands of his classmates.

Now in jest and again in earnest, he is forced to repeat the *confiteor*. One of his essays had been rewarded with the taunt of heresy from his English master, and he takes rueful consolation in the self-conscious part of the Byronic hero. He will not agree that Lord Tennyson is a poet, though he gives tacit consent to the assertion that Newman has the best prose style. But it is his other master, Pater, whose influence is felt at the climax of the chapter. Stephen's sexual initiation is presented in empurpled prose, as an esthetic ritual for which his literary heresies have been preparing him. In trying to find a cadence for his cry, he harks back to the lyricism of *Chamber Music* and the anguish of the small boy in *Dubliners*:[113]

> He stretched out his arms in the street to hold fast the frail swooning form that eluded him and incited him: and the cry that he had strangled for so long in his throat issued from his lips. It broke from him like a wail of despair from a hell of sufferers and died in a wail of furious entreaty, a cry for an iniquitous abandonment, a cry which was but the echo of an obscene scrawl which he had read on the oozing wall of a urinal.

The unromantic reader is prone to feel that a scrawl would have been more adequate to the occasion. The incidence of the word 'swoon' is a humourless symptom of the Pateresque influence on Joyce's early writing. There is many 'A swoon of shame' in *Chamber Music*, and 'a slowly swooning soul' in the last paragraph of *Dubliners*. 'His soul was swooning' at the end of the fourth chapter of the *Portrait of the Artist*, having been darkened by 'the swoon of sin' at the end of the second chapter. Though the scene is clouded with decadent incense, it is clear that Stephen is still a child, and that the woman plays the part of a mother. Joyce's heroes are sons and lovers at the same time; his heroines are always maternal. It is like him to lavish his romantic sensibility on an encounter with a prostitute and to reserve his acrid satire for the domain of the church. In Stephen's mind a symbolic association between art and sex is established, and that precocious revelation helps him to decide his later conflict between art and religion.

Meanwhile, the third chapter is devoted to his remorse. It embodies at formidable length a sermon on hell, suffered by Stephen and his classmates during a retreat. The eloquent Jesuit preacher takes as his object-lesson the sin of Lucifer, pride of the intellect, his great refusal and his terrible fall. Stephen's repentant imagination is harrowed by the torments of the damned. This powerful discourse provides an ethical core for the book, as Father Mapple's sermon on Jonah does for *Moby-Dick*, or Ivan's legend of the Grand Inquisitor for *The Brothers Karamazov*. Joyce is orthodox enough to go on believing in hell, and—as Professor Curtius recognized—to set up his own *Inferno* in *Ulysses*. Like another tormented apostate, Christopher Marlowe, he lives in a world where there is still suffering, but no longer the prospect of salvation. Like Blake's Milton, he is a true poet, and of the devil's party. Stephen's ultimate text is the defiance of the fallen archangel: '*Non serviam!*'

Temporarily, there is confession and absolution. When Stephen sees the eggs and sausages laid out for the communion breakfast, life seems simple and beautiful after all. For a time his restlessness seems to be tranquillized by church and satisfied by school. Seeking to order his existence, he contemplates the possibilities of the Jesuit order itself: the Reverend Stephen Dedalus, S.J. After a conference with a member of that order, he is fascinated and terrified by the awful assumption of powers which ordination involves. In the fourth chapter the call comes unexpectedly—the call to another kind of priesthood. Stephen dedicates himself to art, and enters upon his peculiar novitiate. The church would have meant order, but it would also have meant a denial of the life of the senses. A walk along the strand brings him his real vocation —an outburst of profane joy at the bird-like beauty of a girl, a realization of the fabulous artificer whose name he bears, a consciousness of the power of words to confer an order and life of their own. Like the birds that circle between the sea and the sky, his soul soars in 'an ecstasy of flight', in a metaphor of sexual fulfilment and artistic creation. 'To live, to err, to fall, to triumph, to recreate life out of life!'[196]

The fifth chapter is the discursive chronicle of Stephen's rebellion. He moves among his fellow-students, an aloof and pharisaic figure, unwilling to share their indignation at the first performance of the *Countess Cathleen*, or their confidence in a petition to ensure world peace. His own struggle comes when his mother requests him to make his Easter duty and his diabolic pride of intellect asserts itself. Cranly, with the sharpest instruments of casuistry, tries to probe his stubborn refusal. It is less a question of faith than of observance. Stephen will not, to please his mother, do false homage to the symbols of authority, yet he is not quite un-believer enough to take part in a sacrilegious communion. If he cannot accept the eucharist, he must be anathema; he respects the forms by refusing to observe them. 'I will not serve that in which I no longer believe, whether it call itself my home, my fatherland or my church: and I will try to express myself in some mode of life or art as freely as I can and as wholly as I can, using for my defence the only arms I allow myself to use, silence, exile and cunning.'[281]

With this peremptory gesture, emancipating himself from his petty-bourgeois family, and from Ireland and Catholicism at the same time, Stephen stands ready to take his solitary way wherever the creative life engages him. In a previous argument with other friends, he abandoned the possibility of fighting these issues out at home. 'Ireland is the old sow that eats her farrow.'[231] Davin, the nationalist, is willing to admit that Stephen's position is thoroughly Irish, all too typical of their gifted countrymen. 'In heart you are an Irishman but your pride is too powerful.'[230] Stephen is un-willing to compromise: 'When the soul of a man is born in this country there are nets flung at it to hold it back from flight. You talk to me of nationality, language, religion. I shall try to fly by those nets.' In exile, silence and cunning he trusts to find substi-tutes for those three forms of subjection.

On his way to and from Belvedere College, his soul was 'dis-quieted and cast down by the dull phenomenon of Dublin'.[88] With this realization of the end he was soon to serve, a new vista of 'the slowflowing Liffey' became visible 'across the timeless air'. Nomadic clouds, dappled and seaborne, voyaging westward from Europe, suggested strange tongues and marshalled races.

'He heard a confused music within him as of memories and names. . . .'[191] At University College, the time-worn texts of Ovid and Horace filled him with awe for the past and contempt of the present: '. . . it wounded him to think that he would never be but a shy guest at the feast of the world's culture and that the monkish learning, in terms of which he was striving to forge out an esthetic philosophy, was held no higher by the age he lived in than the subtle and curious jargons of heraldry and falconry.'[207]

English is as strange a tongue as Latin. 'His language, so familiar and so foreign, will always be for me an acquired speech,' Stephen reflects, while conversing with the dean of studies, an English convert to Catholicism. 'I have not made or accepted its words. My voice holds them at bay. My soul frets in the shadow of his language.'[215] The last pages are fragments from Stephen's note-book, duly recording his final interviews with teachers and friends, with his family and 'her'. Spring finds him setting down 'vague words for a vague emotion', his farewell to Dublin, and to sounds of the city which will never stop echoing in his ears:[286]

*April* 10. Faintly, under the heavy night, through the silence of the city which has turned from dreams to dreamless sleep as a weary lover whom no caresses move, the sound of hoofs upon the road.

Toward the end, his purpose stiffens into a flourish of blank verse:[288]

*April* 26. Mother is putting my new secondhand clothes in order. She prays now, she says, that I may learn in my own life and away from home and friends what the heart is and what it feels. Amen. So be it. Welcome, O life! I go to encounter for the millionth time the reality of experience and to forge in the smithy of my soul the uncreated conscience of my race.

On the eve of departure he makes his final entry:

*April* 27. Old father, old artificer, stand me now and ever in good stead.

The mythical and priestly figure of Dædalus is known for more than one work of genius—for a pair of wings, as well as a laby-rinth. Stephen invokes his namesake under both aspects, the hawklike man and the fabulous artificer. Sometimes it is the cunning of the craftsman, the smithy of the artist, that is symbolized. At other times, soaring, falling, flying by the nets of Ireland, it is life itself. Yet these images of aspiration can also be associated with Icarus, the son of Dædalus. That ill-fated and rebellious spirit, who borrowed his father's wings and flew too near the sun, is an equally prophetic symbol: in a classical drama, *Icaro*, the young anti-fascist poet Lauro de Bosis adumbrated the heroism of his own death. The epigraph of Joyce's book is a quotation from Ovid—or rather a misquotation (the correct reference is to the *Metamorphoses*, VIII, 188). Here we are told that Dædalus abandoned his mind to obscure arts, '*et ignotas animum dimittit in artes*'. But Joyce does not tell us Ovid's reason:

> *. . . longumque perosus*
> *exsilium, tractusque soli natalis amore . . .*

The artificer was weary of his long exile and lured by the love of his natal soil, the Roman poet and exile goes on to say, and the rest of his myth rehearses the filial tragedy. The father cries out for the son; Joyce's confused recollection, in *Ulysses*, makes the son cry out for the father: '*Pater, ait.*' On the brink of expatriation, poised for his trial flight, Stephen, in the *Portrait of the Artist*, is more nearly akin to the son. His natural father, Simon Dedalus, is left standing in the mystical kinship of fosterage. The Jesuit fathers, who supervised his education, no longer call him son. He has appealed from Father Dolan to Father Conmee; now he appeals from the church to another paternity. His wings take him from the fatherland. The labyrinth leads toward a father.

# II

---

*The Personal Epic*

# 1. The Two Keys

The publication of *Ulysses* was heralded by a lecture, in which Valery Larbaud confided to the public the main intentions of the book, very much as Joyce had confided them to him. In particular, he pointed out that the title was a key, that the contours of the story would be clear to readers who kept the *Odyssey* in mind, and that an epic conception would impress its form upon the confusing substance of modern life. Other commentators found, however, that not all of Joyce's latent meanings were to be so easily unlocked. Readers who did not happen to be Dubliners felt that Thom's Dublin Directory would make a better guide than Homer. For their benefit, as *A Key to the 'Ulysses' of James Joyce*, Paul Jordan Smith reprinted a map of Dublin. Between these two schools of interpretation there is little room for disagreement; they supplement each other and assist us to comprehend the work as a whole. A single broken phrase, emerging from the last indistinct murmurs of *Finnegans Wake*, is almost an appeal for help: 'The keys to.' We grasp at both keys to *Ulysses*—the map and the myth.

Joyce's Odysseus, an advertising canvasser, exercises his professional wiles in devising a trade-mark for the firm of Alexander J. Keyes. He hits upon Saint Peter's symbol, a pair of crossed keys, also the insignia of the Isle of Man, and thus—if we are willing to follow the implications of a second pun—twin emblems of human isolation. Together they stand for the cross-purposes of the book, its epic symbolism and its naturalistic atmosphere. The one releases the myth-making fantasy of literary tradition; the other reveals a literal-minded itinerary of daily business. We see Stephen Dedalus compelled in a scuffle at the Westland Row

Station to give up his key to the Martello tower, the abandoned
fortification at Sandycove where he has been lodging with Buck
Mulligan—and Dr. Gogarty would have us know that the actual
key was a foot and a half long. We see the canvasser, Leopold
Bloom, promoted in his drunken wish-dream to the high estate of
Lord Mayor of Dublin, and presented with the key to the city.
And afterwards when, in sad sobriety, he invites Stephen to his
home, we note as final evidence of Bloom's ineffectuality that he
has forgotten his latch-key, and must introduce his guest through
the area-way.

The primary object of *Ulysses* is to bring these two inglorious
heroes together, after each has lost his respective key, and to see
whether they have anything to say to each other. All of Joyce's
books, like Thomas Mann's, fit into the broadening dialectical
pattern of *Künstler* versus *Bürger*. In the critical terminology of
Stephen Dedalus, *Ulysses* signalizes a shift from the personal to
the epic; it leads the artist away from himself toward an explora-
tion of the mind of the bourgeois. The form progresses, as Stephen
has foretold, until the centre of emotional gravity is equidistant
between himself and the new hero, Mr. Bloom. But the latter is
not a newcomer to Joyce's mind. As far back as 1906, Joyce had
thought of setting down a full account of the uneventful day of an
ineffectual Mr. Hunter. He first thought of unifying the series of
disjointed sketches, on which he was then engaged, by the title
*Ulysses at Dublin*, instead of *Dubliners*. Meanwhile, he was com-
posing his autobiographical novel, and when he had half completed
the original design for *A Portrait of the Artist as a Young Man*, it
occurred to him that Mr. Hunter's day in Dublin could provide
the occasion for a sequel.

Thus *Ulysses* puts the introspective *Portrait of the Artist* against
the exterior background of *Dubliners*. It might be described as a
desperate effort to reintroduce the artist to his native city. But it
also endeavours to subject the city-dweller to a process of artistic
transfiguration. At the beginning of the Irish revival John Eglinton, in Thoreauistic revolt against the culture of cities, had raised
the question of a new heroic literature. The difficulty, he suggested

in *Pebbles from a Brook*, lay in the unheroic nature of the citizen: '. . . a shell, his power gone from him, civilization like a robe whirled down the stream out of his reach in eddies of London and Paris, the truth no longer the ichor of his being but a cloudy, evaporated mass of problems over his head—this is he, homo sapiens, poor, naked, neurotic, undeceived, ribless wretch—make what you can of him, ye bards!' Joyce could not take up this challenge at once, for he was a schoolboy at the time. For the time, when his English master assigned an essay on 'Your Favourite Hero', he chose to write about Ulysses. Years later, when he was planning his great work, he chose Ulysses for the title role, and rediscovered in ancient myth an archetype for modern man.

His favourite story was still the *Odyssey*, Joyce told a friend, in reaffirming his choice. 'It embodies everything.' The man of many devices, who has known so many men and so many cities, is an all-embracing figure, a composite of the pettiest stratagems and the broadest sympathies in human nature. What a piece of work is a man—the apparition of Ulysses at Dublin prompts us to wonder—ambiguously a ribless wretch exalted to Homeric stature, and a legendary hero fallen upon evil days. Out of these contradictions Joyce's characters derive their special irony and pathos. His epic title, like Galsworthy's *Forsyte Saga*, expresses his reservations. Most of the paladins of realistic fiction, ever since Cervantes made it the literary expression of middle-class culture, have been mock-heroes. Don Quixote's tilts with windmills may, in some Pickwickian sense, have been battles with giants; in the same sense, the trade-route of an Irish canvasser may be the pilgrimage of a contemporary Ulysses. Irish heroes are famous for their long pedigrees. But narrow-minded realism excludes those Mediterranean vistas from the thoroughfares of Dublin, and insists upon scaling a decade of prodigious adventure down to the dimensions of an ordinary day—'the dailiest day possible', in Arnold Bennett's phrase.

On that day, 16th June 1904, the Gold Cup races were run off at Ascot. At New York, when the *General Slocum* exploded in the East River, five hundred lives were lost. From the Orient came news of Russo-Japanese conflict over Port Arthur. Nothing in particular happened in Ireland; Dublin remained the centre of paralysis. The weather was fair, and warmer in the afternoon, with thunder in the evening, and showers at night. At the Gaiety Theatre Mrs. Bandman Palmer was appearing in *Leah*. At the Queen's the Elster-Grimes Opera Company was performing *The Lily of Killarney*. Handbills, floating about the city, announced the coming of an American evangelist, J. Alexander Dowie. Clery's was advertising a summer sale; sandwich-men, bearing the more or less consecutive letters of H.E.L.Y.'S., filed through the streets. In schools and churches, libraries and newspaper offices, shops and concert-halls, public-houses and houses of prostitution, there was business as usual.

In the morning, at Glasnevin Cemetery, the body of one Patrick Dignam is buried. At midnight, in the maternity hospital on Holles Street, a child is born to a Mrs. Mina Purefoy. Leopold Bloom is a passive spectator at both these events. He plays an even less active part in the event which takes place that afternoon in his own home at 7 Eccles Street, when his wife, the singer, Mme Marion Tweedy Bloom, commits adultery with her concert-manager, Hugh E. ('Blazes') Boylan. Nor is the day a much more eventful one in the life of Stephen Dedalus. His six months of exile in Paris abruptly terminated with five momentous words: 'Mother dying come home father.'[39] Now he is living in the Martello tower, and teaching in the private school of Mr. Garret Deasy at Dalkey. After his quarrel with Mulligan, he decides not to return to Sandycove; he tells an unemployed stranger that there will be a job at Dalkey next day, and walks homeward with Mr. Bloom. But he soon leaves his new friend and goes his own way. The decision of this indecisive day is for each of them to continue—Stephen as an exile, Bloom as a Dubliner.

Such intermingling of private lives and public routines does not often ask for heroic treatment. To amplify the subject of the city, as Balzac discovered, is to dwarf its inhabitants: he made the metropolis his actual hero, or rather villain, by investing Louis-Philippe's Paris with the sinister glamour of Haroun-al-Raschid's

Baghdad or Dante's *Inferno*. Dickens and Dostoevsky were more concerned with penetrating into humble existences, by listening through partitions and looking down skylights in tenements and lodging-houses, but neither could dispense with the treacherous aid of melodrama. Joyce was somewhat susceptible to melodrama, but he managed to sublimate it—in the psychological crises of both Stephen and Bloom—to a highly subjective plane. He would not even use history, as Hugo and Tolstoy had done, to lend epic magnitude to an urban theme; they threw their heroes into bold relief, by allowing Jean Valjean to carry Marius through the foul sewers of Paris, or Pierre Bezuhov to rescue a scrofulous child from the smoking ruins of Moscow. In contrast to these gigantic protagonists, Mr. Bloom, extricating Stephen from a brawl with two British privates and hurrying him off to a cabman's shelter for a cup of coffee and rolls, is inconspicuous and pitiable.

Always evasive when confronted by action, Joyce shuns heroics. The relation of the *Odyssey* to *Ulysses* is that of parallels which never meet. The Homeric overtones do contribute their note of universality, their range of tradition, to what might well be a trivial and colourless tale. But in so doing, they convert a realistic novel into a mock-epic. The present is treated as a travesty of the past; richness furnishes an ironic comment on reality. So, in Mr. Eliot's mock-epic of latter-day London, the spectacle of Queen Elizabeth in her barge of state is obscured by the smoke of the coal barges on a later and murkier Thames. Life is not less real, to Joyce, for being completely divorced from storied splendour. Heroic deeds are one thing, and daily chores are another, and he is careful to keep them in different spheres. The sphere of the city is the habitual and the commonplace. Perhaps this assumption will do more than anything else to date Joyce's work. Few imaginative writers since Flaubert, as Edmund Wilson demonstrates, have been willing to concede a sense of glory to their own times. But times change, and the established routines of city life are interrupted by air-raid sirens.

The occasion of the *Odyssey*, though it remains a matter of dark reminiscence, is the fall of a city. It is a story of exile and, after a long circuit of misadventures, homecoming. It is a vital, though belated, part of the most recurrent cycle of European legend: many nations trace their ancestry to the sons of Priam, and Neo-Platonic criticism viewed the peregrinations of Odysseus as an allegory of the soul. Stephen's temporary employer, Mr. Deasy, viewed the role of Kitty O'Shea in the fall of Parnell as that which Helen had played in the fall of Troy. The pastime of finding classical precedents for modern instances held its attraction for Joyce, and after a fashion he carries out Mulligan's glib scheme for Hellenizing Ireland. The closeness of the correspondences between his Irish characters and their Hellenic prototypes is a point that can be, and has been, heavily laboured. Not everything in *Ulysses* has its avatar in the *Odyssey*, needless to say, nor have the sequence and emphasis of the ancient epic been preserved. The reader of Joyce who turns back to Homer is more struck by divergences than by analogies.

The principal adventures of the wily Odysseus are narrated retrospectively, and the interest is concentrated upon the drama of his return to his island kingdom. Four introductory books describe the efforts of the son, Telemachus, to seek out his father. Only with the next four do we see Odysseus *en voyage*, from Ogygia where he has been staying for seven years with the nymph Calypso, to Phaeacia where he recounts his wanderings to the credulous ears of the court of Nausicaa's father. This indirect narration of his most spectacular exploits occupies only four books more. The last twelve, which comprise the second half of the *Odyssey*, are devoted to the arrival at Ithaca and the reunion with Penelope. The most offhand comparison of the successive women in the lives of Odysseus and Bloom will illustrate how freely Joyce has handled this material. Calypso is not Molly Bloom, though Bloom naturally rises from her bed; she is the invisible Martha Clifford, a typist with whom he is carrying on a surreptitious correspondence. The encounter with Nausicaa, otherwise Gerty MacDowell, comes late in the day and carries all too little consequence. The encounter with Circe, *alias* Bella Cohen, instead of being part of a shadowy flashback, is the climax of the book. And

Molly is the faithful Penelope with a difference that is one of the most fertile sources of Joyce's irony.

Joyce's irony—he never lets us forget—is two-edged, and is constantly cutting back to the sources of his pathos. The immediate effect of this method, we have seen, is to reduce his characters to mock-heroic absurdity. A further and quite contradictory effect is to magnify them, to treat their little habits as profound rituals, to attach a universal significance to the most minute particulars. 'The business of the poet or novelist', Thomas Hardy noted, 'is to show the sorriness of the grandest things and the grandeur of the sorriest things.' Joyce's use of detail is the concrete link between naturalism and symbolism, the end product of a twofold process of reproduction and selection, which supplies the book with both local colour and ulterior meaning. Stephen is still watching for a sign, a shading, an unexpected epiphany: 'Signatures of all things I am here to read. . . .'[33] They may be the merest *minutiæ*; within the limited range of history they may seem ephemeral and slight; but in the wider orbit of nature they have their appointed function. The humblest object or crudest incident is a microcosm which may contain a key to the secrets of that wider universe.[31]

—History, Stephen said, is a nightmare from which I am trying to awake.

From the playfield the boys raised a shout. A whirring whistle: goal. What if that nightmare gave you a back kick?

—The ways of the Creator are not our ways, Mr Deasy said. All history moves towards one great goal, the manifestation of God.

Stephen jerked his thumb towards the window, saying:

—That is God.

Hooray! Ay! Whrrwhee!

—What? Mr Deasy asked.

—A shout in the street, Stephen answered, shrugging his shoulders.

The student who demands a philosophy from Joyce will be put off with an inarticulate noise and a sceptical shrug. '*Du sagst nichts und verrätst nichts, O Ulysses, aber du wirkst!*' exclaims Dr. Jung. A novel is tested by its reality, and not by its message. Association, not logic, is the motive power of Joyce's mentality; he plays with ideas as with words. When Mrs. Bloom worries her husband with the polysyllabic mysteries of 'metempsychosis', or when Stephen conceives the notion of an umbilical telephone line to Edenville, they are simply asserting their sense of the past, of the recurrence and continuity of human experience. Joyce does not preach, any more than Donne, the transmigration of souls. His readers, like Donne's, must be ready to distinguish between occult beliefs and metaphysical conceits. They must know the difference between doctrines and attitudes. Any given system of ideas—even the eclectic make-believe of Yeats's *Vision*—would have cramped Joyce. He was anxious to take all knowledge for his playground.

Scholiasts, those who have taken Joyce for their playground, push their game to an Alexandrian extreme. Joyce, no doubt, has given them every temptation and encouragement. Yet, when Stuart Gilbert informs us that each episode of *Ulysses* has not only its Homeric antecedent, but also its own organ of the body, its characteristic colour, and a plethora of other symbols, we find ourselves approaching it gingerly, like Charlie Chaplin chewing a pudding in which a coin has been embedded. We are pleased with ourselves and Joyce and Mr. Gilbert, if Bloom broils an explicit kidney for breakfast or 'green thought in a green shade' tinctures Stephen's seaside meditations. If the symbols are more extrinsic, we are less pleased; and if they are entirely out of sight, we seldom miss them. They are not there for us, but for Joyce. They are not evidences of esoteric philosophy, but of intricate technique. Utterly unshackled from the usual conventions, Joyce hedged himself in with far more complicated conditions and far more rigorous restrictions than any school of criticism would ever dare to exact.

It is not difficult to imagine the licensed premises of Barney Kiernan as a kind of Cyclops' cave; it is enlightening to regard the enraged Sinn Feiner who attacks our hero as a Polyphemus *de nos jours*; and it is entertaining to learn, from the authorized insight of Mr. Gilbert, that there are glimmerings of the olive-wood club of Odysseus in the fiery tip of Mr. Bloom's 'knock-medown cigar'. In some respects, the Homeric parallel is a useful contrivance for the reader. By giving him something to take for granted and showing him something to look for, by helping him to control an overwhelming flux of impressions, it justifies its existence. In other respects, it seems more important to Joyce than it could possibly be to any reader. Mr. Deasy's preoccupations with the foot-and-mouth disease, it seems, alludes to one of Joyce's journalistic ventures, as well as to Nestor's sacrifice of a heifer. The myth may well have served as a scaffolding, while Joyce constructed his work. Before it was printed, he tacitly removed the Homeric chapter headings that appear in the manuscript.

Since they resolve the book into such a transparent outline, in Joyce's own terms, it is convenient to reprint them here. They reveal, more graphically than further discussion or second-hand summary, how the myth of the *Odyssey* is superimposed upon the map of Dublin, how the retelling of an old fable is absorbed into the cross-section of a contemporary city. Joyce has rearranged the twenty-four books of Homer in three parts, subdivided into eighteen episodes of increasing length and elaboration. The first three constitute a prologue, more or less equivalent to the first four books of the *Odyssey*, the so-called *Telemachia*. In Joyce's personal epic, they effect the transition between the *Portrait of the Artist* and *Ulysses*. Stephen is now identified with Telemachus: his new name signifies 'away from war', and his continuing quest is for a father who was in the battle.

I. 1. *Telemachus*. 8 A.M. Breakfast at the Martello tower.[1]
   2. *Nestor*. 10 A.M. A history lesson at Mr. Deasy's school.[21]
   3. *Proteus*. 11 A.M. A walk along the beach at Sandymount.[33]

The body of the book consists of the twelve subsequent episodes, always expanding and often reversing the eight books into which Homer has concentrated the wanderings of Odysseus. The emphasis has shifted back from the return, which is necessarily attenuated in Joyce's version, to the exile. The first public engagement, the funeral procession to Glasnevin Cemetery, reproduces the trip to Hades, which was one of the last incidents on the voyage of the wily Greek. Mr. Bloom's erratic route, from breakfast until midnight, manages to find some local landmark for every one of his predecessor's stopping-places in the cradle of civilization. When his fatigued imagination, at the end of the day, conjures up a chorus of daughters of Erin, their litany is a recital of his negligible exploits, and a running commentary on the central episodes of the book.[474]

II. 1. *Calypso.* 8 A.M. Breakfast at 7 Eccles Street.[48]

Kidney of Bloom, pray for us.

2. *Lotus Eaters.* 10 A.M. The public baths (and a phallic symbol).[63]

Flower of the Bath, pray for us.

3. *Hades.* 11 A.M. At the funeral (with an eminent solicitor).[79]

Mentor of Menton, pray for us.

4. *Æolus.* Noon. At the office of his newspaper.[108]

Canvasser for the Freeman, pray for us.

5. *Lestrygonians.* 1 P.M. Lunch at Davy Byrne's pub.[139]

Charitable Mason, pray for us.

6. *Scylla and Charybdis.* 2 P.M. Bloom in library (soap in pocket).[172]

Wandering Soap, pray for us.

7. *Wandering Rocks.* 3 P.M. The streets and the bookstall.[206]

Sweets of Sin, pray for us.

8. *Sirens.* 4 P.M. Barmaids at the Ormond Hotel.[242]

Music without Words, pray for us.

9. *Cyclops.* 5 P.M. Humiliation at Barney Kiernan's.[277]

Reprover of the Citizen, pray for us.

10. *Nausicaa.* 8 P.M. Flirtation with Gerty MacDowell.[329]

Friend of all Frillies, pray for us.

11. *Oxen of the Sun.* 10 P.M. The maternity hospital.[366]
Midwife Most Merciful, pray for us.

12. *Circe.* Midnight. Bella Cohen's brothel (Bloom's amulet).[410]
Potato Preservative against Plague and Pestilence, pray for us.

In so far as the story is Bloom's, this time-table is reliable. A notable exception is the library scene, where he cuts a dim and transient figure while Stephen holds the floor. Stephen, for the most part, is conspicuous by his absence until the evening episodes. The third section serves as an epilogue, corresponding to the *Nostos*, or homecoming, in the last twelve books of the *Odyssey*. Though it includes the long-awaited dialogue between Bloom and Stephen, the predominating figure is finally Molly Bloom. This is her part of the book, as the first is Stephen's, and the second Bloom's.

III. 1. *Eumæus.* 1 A.M. The cabman's shelter.[575]
2. *Ithaca.* 2 A.M. 7 Eccles Street: the kitchen.[626]
3. *Penelope.* 2.45 A.M. 7 Eccles Street: the bedroom.[698]

The architectural framework, which Joyce reconstructed from Homer, is most impressive when we contemplate the work as a whole and try to visualize the relation of its parts. When we turn from the structure to the texture, we are more easily persuaded to think of musical forms. The sonata, Ezra Pound insists, is a clearer model than the epic. Its introductory theme would be Stephen, its main theme Bloom; each, after a preliminary exposition, undergoes his own development, then a treatment in combination, and at last a recapitulation. Since the first three episodes of the first section are cleverly synchronized with the first three of the second, Bloom and Stephen do not begin to cross each other's paths until midday. At eight-forty-five precisely, the same little cloud hides the sun from Stephen in his tower[7] and from Bloom on his walk home from the butcher-shop.[54] Their morning hours are presented

75

in isolation, and they are again isolated by the morning hours of the next day.

The two years that have elapsed since the conclusion of the *Portrait of the Artist* have done much to sharpen Stephen's mind, but nothing to change it. The savour of the Latin Quarter and the disintegration of his family seem to confirm his original decision. So long as he must remain in Dublin, the rebellious archangel continues to loom before his mind's eye: 'Allbright he falls, proud lightning of the intellect.'[47] We follow Stephen's ramblings with a growing conviction that this is not homecoming, but an interruption of exile. True, he has tried his wings; he sometimes feels that he has fallen into the sea; frequently he dwells upon the sea-changed images of death by water. He is preoccupied with the lapwing, the emblematic bird that safeguards its children by crying away from its nest. If he is still Icarus, who, where, is Dædalus? When John Eglinton suggests that the name may have some bearing on his 'fantastical humour', Stephen is touched by a pang of reminiscence:[199]

Fabulous artificer, the hawklike man. You flew. Whereto? Newhaven-Dieppe, steerage passenger. Paris and back. Lapwing. Icarus. *Pater, ait.* Seabedabbled, fallen, weltering. Lapwing you are. Lapwing he.

Misunderstanding has become tragedy with the death of his mother. Throughout the day, from the early moment when Mulligan addresses the sea in Hellenic phrase as 'our mighty mother', Stephen is haunted by the vision of her wasted body in its grave-clothes, and the odour of wax and rosewood and wetted ashes. The prayer which stuck in his throat at her death-bed, with its radiant evocation of the welcoming hosts of heaven, repeats itself over and over: *Liliata rutilantium te confessorum turma circumdet: iubilantium te virginum chorus excipiat.* Self-reproach takes the quaint form of a Middle English expression for remorse of conscience, 'Agenbite of Inwit'; again and again, within his mind, we feel its mordant impact. At school he perplexes his pupils with the declension of *amor matris*. All occasions inform against him; all reflection is darkly tinged with repressed accusations that material-ize among the bitter ghosts of midnight.

Though Stephen's nature has not radically altered, Joyce's characterization throws new light upon it, and examines it for the first time 'in mediate relation to others'. A freer orientation, transcending the narrow limits of egotism, has enabled him to paint a more objective self-portrait. As his own youth receded, he was able to take a long-range view of 'the artist as a young man', for better or for worse, with maturity and even humour. When Stephen seems as priggish to the reader as to the bumptious Mulligan, and when Mulligan seems more of a good fellow to the reader than to Stephen, we must acknowledge that Joyce has gone a long way toward detachment. There are still certain adverbial distinctions between Stephen's innate refinement and the vulgarity of the rest of the world: his speeches are spoken 'coldly', Mulligan's 'coarsely'. This, perhaps, is the conscious outcome of self-dramatization. When Mulligan apologizes for a coarse remark, 'O, it's only Dedalus whose mother is beastly dead,' Stephen replies, coldly:[7]

—I am not thinking of the offence to my mother.
—Of what, then? Buck Mulligan asked.
—Of the offence to me, Stephen answered.
Buck Mulligan swung round on his heel.
—O, an impossible person! he exclaimed.

The *Portrait of the Artist* has already familiarized us with the cast of Stephen's mind. A chance phrase of the newspaper editor, Myles Crawford, 'I see it in your face,' reminds him—as it reminds us—of the indelible words of Father Dolan and the old *traumata* of Clongowes Wood: 'See it in your eye. Lazy idle little schemer.'[126] Among the later confusions of the brothel, the prefect of studies, armed with his pandybat, emerges like a jack-in-the-box from the pianola.[531] Afterwards, as Mr. Bloom guides Stephen's faltering steps past Baird's stone-cutting works, we recall those private associations between various quarters of Dublin and Stephen's literary enthusiasms, and we think of Ibsen. So, in spite of his intoxication, does Stephen.[576] Bloom's mind is a brighter mirror of the world around them. It reflects sense impressions concretely, whereas Stephen is continually refracting them through speculation and introspection. At Sandymount, as each of them covers the same ground, contrasting soliloquies balance 'the intellectual imagination' of Stephen in the morning against the carnal susceptibilities of Bloom in the evening. The latter is so mobile, so suggestible, so easily distracted, that his thought is hard to dissociate from his terrain. He can claim, with Tennyson's *Ulysses*, 'I am a part of all that I have met.'

As we take our leave of Telemachus, sauntering along the strand with his ashplant, and catch our earliest glimpse of Ulysses, getting his wife's breakfast and putting out milk for the cat, we pass from the intransigent intellectual to the *homme sensuel moyen*. Stephen, if not all spirit, is bent upon humbling his flesh. Bloom's first recorded reaction is his obvious physical relish for 'the inner organs of beasts and fowls'. His consistent earthiness, which does not spare us the intimacies of the stool or the bath, makes *Ulysses* one of the few books that attaches to animal functions the same importance that they have in life. Not that Bloom lacks intelligence, for he is shrewd and sensitive. 'There's a touch of the artist about old Bloom,' Lenehan says to M'Coy.[222] There is just enough of the frustrated artist to draw him to Stephen and Stephen in turn is drawn to Bloom by these very frustrations, since Bloom has accepted so much that he has rejected. He is seeking a father; Bloom has lost a son. They are complementary figures, and each is one-sided and maladjusted so long as he abides alone. Yet the attraction of opposites is not enough to produce a synthesis.

An Irish Jew, indeed, is a walking antithesis. Mr. Deasy has paved the way for Bloom's entrance with his little joke: Ireland is the one country that has never persecuted the Jews, because she never let them in. England is dying, in the opinion of Mr. Deasy, an Orangeman, because she is in their hands. 'And they are the signs of a nation's decay.'[30] And Stephen, listening, seems to see the dark eyes and eager gestures of patient wanderers in the ghettoes and on the stock-exchanges of Europe. The question of why Joyce chose a Jew for his hero—which Valery Larbaud raised, but did not answer—has answered itself. From Proust's Swann to Mann's Joseph, Jewish figures have received a disproportionate amount of consideration from contemporary novelists. The influence, variously manifested, of Marx in politics, Bergson in philosophy, Freud in the humane sciences, and Einstein in the mathematical sciences, has lent a semblance of plausibility to the argument of those critics of modern culture who would convict it of a non-Aryan taint.

Whether the Jews be chosen people or bearers of the curse, they have a special affinity with an Irish author who dates his book from '*Trieste—Zürich—Paris*'. Besides Mr. Hunter of Dublin, who must have been an Anglo-Irishman, we hear of other models for Mr. Bloom—a Greek in Trieste, a Hungarian in Zürich, the Austro-Italian writer Italo Svevo, and possibly members of an Italian Jewish household in which Joyce had lived. In any case, his hero would be a metropolitan type, neither a native nor a foreigner, a denizen of the megalopolis, a wanderer of the diaspora, equally at home and ill at ease in any city of the world. Mulligan calls Bloom the wandering Jew. 'I fear thee, ancient mariner.'[206] Professor Lowes has confirmed this identification, by discerning the features of the same restless pilgrim in the garb of Coleridge's bright-eyed seafarer. 'Ahasuerus I call him,' snarls the Sinn Feiner. 'Cursed by God.'[322] Joyce, by accepting Victor Bérard's theory of the Semitic origins of the *Odyssey*, identifies Bloom with an even more ancient mariner, and links Homer with the Bible.

Bloom is an exile in Dublin, as Stephen is a Dubliner in exile. Before breakfast, musing on the attrition and corruption of the cities of the plain, he walks to the pork-butcher's, where surprisingly he picks up a prospectus for a Zionistic settlement. This stimulates him, from time to time, to escape from the waste land about him into tropical reveries of the promised land. The address of the project, Bleibtreustrasse, Berlin, carries its ironic reprimand, for he has not remained true to the religion of his fathers. He has not continued to observe the protestant religion of his mother, into which he has been baptized. He has gone, like Stephen, into spiritual exile. In Babylon he remembers Zion. When he brings back his pork kidney, he notices that there is a letter to his wife from Boylan, and realizes that there will be an informal rehearsal of 'Love's Old Sweet Song' at his home that afternoon. This *leit-motif* of his wife's infidelity cuts him off from his family, just as relentlessly as Stephen is cut off by his mother's death-bed prayer.

Isolated together, Joyce sets his personification of the city alongside of his portrait of the artist. Neither is complete without the other, he knew very well, but he also knew that both are usually incomplete. He succeeded in uniting them by a literary *tour de force*, by crossing the two keys of topography and mythology. Bloom, however, is unaware of his symbolic role, just as Stephen is out of touch with his municipal environment. Stephen starts as an individual and becomes a type. Bloom starts as a type and becomes an individual. One by critical precept, the other by awful example, mark the distance between culture and philistinism. Matthew Arnold, though painfully conscious of this distance, might not have recognized them as unhonoured prophets of Hellenism and Hebraism. The strains and stresses of middle-class life have alienated Stephen and vulgarized Bloom, have introverted the Hellene and extraverted the Hebrew. Still, somewhere between Stephen's esthetic feeling and Bloom's civic sense, between individual expression and social morality, lies our only hope for the good life. 'Hebraism and Hellenism,' Arnold has written, '—between these two points of influence moves our world. At one time it feels more powerfully the attraction of one of them, at another time of the other; and it ought to be, though it never is, evenly and happily balanced between them.'

# 2. Montage

The imitation of life through the medium of language has never been undertaken more literally. *Ulysses* ignores the customary formalities of narration and invites us to share a flux of undifferentiated experience. We are not told how the characters behave; we are confronted with the *stimuli* that affect their behaviour, and expected to respond sympathetically. The act of communication, the bond of sympathy which identifies the reader with the book, comes almost too close for comfort. The point of view, the principle of form which has served to integrate many amorphous novels, is intimate and pervasive. Joyce's efforts to achieve immediacy lead him to equate form and content, to ignore the distinction between the things he is describing and the words he is using to describe them. In this equation, time is of the essence. Events are reported when and as they occur; the tense is a continuous present. Joyce did not begin his *Portrait of the Artist*, as other autobiographers would, by summoning up a retrospective account of his earliest remembrances. Instead, the opening pages of the book are presented as an exact verbal equivalent of the opening impressions of his life.

The story of *Ulysses* takes no longer to happen than to read; acting time, as it were, is simultaneous with reading time. The plot of the novel is Mr. Bloom's schedule, which introduces us to divers places in Dublin at consecutive periods of the day. We have observed that Bloom's day lasts for sixteen waking hours, with some intermissions and interpolations, prefaced by a separate treatment of Stephen's morning and concluded with a tardy glimpse of Molly Bloom—eighteen hours and forty-five minutes by the final page. Bloom, on the whole, is our sensorium, and it is his experience that becomes ours. To record this experience, however, has not been a simple process of photography. Bloom's mind is neither a *tabula rasa* nor a photographic plate, but a motion picture, which has been ingeniously cut and carefully edited to emphasize the close-ups and fade-outs of flickering emotion, the angles of observation and the flashbacks of reminiscence. In its intimacy and in its continuity, *Ulysses* has more in common with the cinema than with other fiction. The movement of Joyce's style, the thought of his characters, is like unreeling film; his method of construction, the arrangement of this raw material, involves the crucial operation of *montage*.

Joyce's unrewarded attempt to establish the first motion-picture theatre in Ireland is only another chapter in the history of his misunderstandings with his country, but he fully understood the technical possibilities of the new medium. He keenly perceived—in spite of his defective vision—that the cinema is both a science and an art, and therefore the most characteristic expression of our time. His own technique shows the confluence of many modern developments in the arts and sciences. The impressionistic painters, by defining their object through the eyes of the beholder, gave Joyce an example which his physical handicap may have encouraged him to follow. The 'ineluctable modality of the visible' was narrowed down for him, so that blurred sight looked for compensation in augmented sound. The Wagnerian school, with its thematic blend of music and ideas, had its obvious lesson for a novelist who had wanted to be a lyric poet or a professional singer.

The international psychoanalytic movement, under the direction of Jung, had its headquarters in Zürich during the war years while Joyce was writing *Ulysses*, and he could scarcely have resisted its influence. And, although philosophy could not have offered him much in the way of immediate data, it is suggestive to note that Bergson, Whitehead, and others—by reducing things-in-themselves to a series of organic relations—were thinking in the same direction. Thus the very form of Joyce's book is an elusive and eclectic *Summa* of its age: the *montage* of the cinema, impressionism in painting, *leitmotif* in music, the free association of psychoanalysis, and vitalism in philosophy. Take of these elements all that is fusible, and perhaps more, and you have the style of *Ulysses*. To characterize this style, we must borrow a term from either German metaphysics or French rhetoric; we may conceive it as *Strom des Bewusstseins* or again as *monologue intérieur*. We shall find, however, that Joyce obtains his metaphysical effects by rhetorical devices, that the internal monologue lends itself more readily to critical analysis than the more illusory stream of consciousness.

The emergence of this method in fiction has been hailed as nothing less than a scientific discovery, and attributed to a half-remembered French symbolist, Edouard Dujardin. Joyce himself generously acknowledged his debt to a short novel of Dujardin's, *Les lauriers sont coupés*, first published in 1887 and reprinted in the afterglow of Joyce's acknowledgement. Dujardin was not utterly unknown to the Dublin of *Ulysses*, since *Dana: A Magazine of Independent Thought* carried his defence of the excommunicated Catholic historian, Alfred Loisy, a month before Stephen tried to persuade the editor, John Eglinton, to accept an article on Shakespeare. The elderly innovator survived to promulgate a rambling definition of the style which he had invented and Joyce had perfected: 'The internal monologue, in its nature on the order of poetry, is that unheard and unspoken speech by which a character expresses his inmost thoughts (those lying nearest the unconscious) without regard to logical organizations—that is, in their original state—by means of direct sentences reduced to the syntactic minimum, and in such a way as to give the impression of reproducing the thoughts just as they come into the mind.'

Dujardin's original experiment is something less than sensational. *Les lauriers sont coupés* is the sustained monologue in the present tense, without incident or consequence, of a naïve young man taking a beautiful actress out to dinner, interrupted by occasional fragments of dialogue and a few necessary stage-directions in the first person. The little book did not escape the sharp eye of Remy de Gourmont, who reviewed it as 'a novel which seems in literature a transposed anticipation of the cinema'. It seems to bear the same relation to ordinary fiction that the film does to the stage. For, to find ample literary precedent for the internal monologue, we need only turn to the theatre. The conventions of Elizabethan drama permitted Shakespeare to marshal the arguments for and against suicide in Hamlet's soliloquy, or to mingle desperation with prose and song in the distractions of Ophelia's madness. Recent playwrights, like Eugene O'Neill, have renewed their licence to soliloquize. Poets like Browning and T. S. Eliot have never abandoned this prerogative.

Even within the traditions of the novel, the internal monologue appears to be less of an innovation than Joyce or Dujardin would have liked to believe. André Gide has found instances in Dostoevsky's *House of the Dead.* Fanny Burney wrote tolerably conventional novels, a hundred years before Dostoevsky or Dujardin, but in the privacy of her diary she set down a page or two that ask demurely for comparison with the last words of Molly Bloom:

Well, I am going to bed—Sweet dreams attend me—and may you sympathize with me. Heigh ho! I wonder when I shall return to London!— Not that we are very dull here—no, really—tolerably happy—I wish Kitty Cooke would write to me—I long to hear how my dear, dear, beloved Mr. Crisp does. My papa always mentions him by the name of my *Flame.* Indeed he is not mistaken—himself is the *only* man on earth I prefer to him. Well—I must write a word more—only to end my paper—so!—that's done—and now good night to you . . . . . .

James Fenimore Cooper, one of the least adroit novelists who ever won lasting fame, somehow flounders into the stream of consciousness. Cooper follows Scott in taking over a Shakespearian *entourage* of clowns and fools, one of whom is an old Negro retainer, Caesar, in *The Spy.* When his young master takes leave of him, and jocosely suggests that Caesar convey a farewell kiss to the young ladies of the household, Cooper's racial feeling sinks into Caesar's subconsciousness:

The delighted Caesar closed the door, pushing bolt after bolt, and turning the key until it would turn no more, soliloquizing the whole time on the happy escape of his young master.

'How well he ride—teach him good deal myself—salute a young lady —Miss Fanny wouldn't let the old coloured man kiss a red cheek.'

This staccato diction, as the malice of Wyndham Lewis did not fail to observe, makes a startling appearance in the very first novel of Charles Dickens. *Pickwick Papers* is ordinarily evoked for other qualities than psychological subtlety. There are moments, none the less, when it would be hard to tell the silent meditation of Mr. Bloom from the laconic garrulity of Alfred Jingle, Esq. The flow of Mr. Jingle's discourse is also stimulated by the sight of local landmarks, and the movement of the stage-coach is registered in his spoken reactions:

'Terrible place—dangerous work—other day—five children—mother— tall lady, eating sandwiches—forgot the arch—crash—knock—children look around—mother's head off—sandwich in her hand—no mouth to put in—head of a family off—shocking, shocking! Looking at Whitehall, sir?—fine place—little window—somebody's else's head off there, eh, sir?—he didn't keep a sharp look-out enough either—eh, sir, eh?'

Herman Melville's hero, in *Moby-Dick*, is not psychoanalysed but dramatized. Yet Ahab, lonely and absolute, scanning the sea from his cabin at sunset, has a curious resemblance to Stephen, in his self-conscious soliloquy by the shore. Their gestures are alike, if their speeches differ, and the difference is primarily a question of rhetoric. Ahab's speeches tend to fall into the natural metre of English tragedy:

> What I've dared, I've willed;
> and what I've willed, I'll do! They think me mad—
> Starbuck does; but I'm demoniac,
> I am madness maddened! That wild madness
> that's only calm to comprehend itself!
> The prophecy was that I should be dismembered;
> and—Aye! I lost this leg. I now prophesy
> that I will dismember my dismemberer.
> Now, then, be the prophet and the fulfiller one.
> That's more than ye, ye great gods, ever were.

It is no more true to say of Joyce, than of any other artist, that his work enlarges the domain of consciousness. *Ulysses* demonstrates no more about the processes of the mind than *Les Rougon-Macquart* proves about the laws of heredity. It is no service to Joyce to insist that his book is a scientific demonstration, and no disservice to recognize that his real originality is firmly grounded in literary tradition. We are so dazzled by the consummate craftsmanship that we forget to watch the conscientious craftsman. Though he may be more facile and complex than other writers, he conforms to the standards of their common craft. Though *Ulysses* employs the resources of the language to the extent of 29,899 different words, over half of these appear only once, and many of the rest serve some special purpose that seldom requires them to be repeated. Almost half of the 260,430 words in the book are drawn from a basic vocabulary of about a hundred monosyllables, which—as Professor Hanley and his associates have shown in their index—closely coincide with the norms of colloquial usage. Occasionally there is a significant displacement: the word 'street' is far more frequent in *Ulysses* than in ordinary speech. On the other hand, 'is' and various verbal auxiliaries, because of the telegraphic syntax of internal monologue, are relatively infrequent with Joyce.

Joyce's habits of composition were Dædalean labours, to which his rewritten manuscripts and revised proofs bear formidable testimony. Collation of a casual page of printer's typescript with the final text of *Ulysses* indicates that sixty-five corrections have been made in proof—most of them mechanical details, to be sure, but at least ten contributions of some importance. There is little erasure or retrenchment; there is always addition, but never subtraction. Afterthought furnishes some of the most salient touches. For example, the mocking repetition in the Circe episode of Mulligan's taunt, 'She's beastly dead,'[547] was pencilled in shortly before the typescript reached the printer. In some cases Joyce kept revising even after periodical publication. He could scarcely have composed his work by any other method than persistent accretion. He had first to compile an exhaustive and matter-of-fact *dossier*, on the plane of objective description that comes to the surface only in the Ithaca episode of the book; then to redistribute this material, with coloured crayons and other mechanical aids, planting associations in the stream of consciousness and laying down coincidences according to his two keys; and finally to hope that this man-made chaos would synthesize in the reader's mind.

The exposition of *Ulysses* is necessarily circular; it plunges the reader, with epic vengeance, *in medias res*. Jung has declared that it has neither a beginning nor an end, that it can be read both forwards and backwards. The reader, entering the minds of the characters without the formality of an introduction, will encounter allusions long before they are explained. When Bloom puts on his hat to leave his house in the morning, he manifests concern over a slip of paper inside his hat-band.[49] Later, at the post office, we discover that this card contains the *nom de plume*, Henry Flower, under which he is secretly corresponding with Martha Clifford.[63] Throughout the remainder of the book, the partly obliterated trade name inside the hat-band, 'Plasto's high grade ha', becomes synonymous with Bloom's adulterous impulses.[265] Stephen's reactions are more imaginative, but equally furtive. When he meets his sister, Dilly, in a book-stall, he feels a painful sense of the decline of his family since their mother's death. The haunting image of his mother does not figure directly in his thoughts; self-reproach has found a purely verbal substitution:[230]

> She is drowning. Agenbite. Save her. Agenbite. All against us. She will drown me with her, eyes and hair. Lank coils of seaweed hair around me, my heart, my soul. Salt green death.
> We.
> Agenbite of inwit. Inwit's agenbite.
> Misery! Misery!

Joyce's literary sensibilities have endowed such passages with a peculiar poignance—not less peculiar nor poignant because they are difficult to communicate. That he should have seen fit to envelop the most genuine emotion in his book with the title of a treatise on the seven deadly sins by a fourteenth-century monk, Dan Michel of Northgate, carries mere pedantry to the point of paranoia. Bloom's psychology is coarser than Stephen's, but not less literary. As an advertising man, he is a man of letters in a small way. In lascivious mood, he conceives himself as Raoul, hero of the pornographic novel, *Sweets of Sin*; his messianic conscience addresses him as Elijah, straight off the handbill of the evangelist Dowie. Joyce's psychology is based on the *idée-fixe*, and tagged to appropriate echoes for every context. Ideas are put into words, and verbal themes are set to music. The note of blasphemy upon which the book opens, Mulligan's parody of the mass, is stridently repeated when Stephen enters the brothel. A whole liturgy is associated with the death of Mrs. Dedalus, and Bloom's cuckoldry is intermittently rehearsed in gems from his wife's operatic repertory. Church and state are celebrated in the ribald ballads of 'Joking Jesus' and 'Coronation Day'. The texture of the internal monologue derives its richness and stiffness from a continuous thread of quotation.

We remember Stephen as a lyrical youth, trying his magic by attaching phrases to feelings. The pity of it, we remember, lay in the failure of words like 'Araby' and 'Grace' to cover the situations of *Dubliners*. We know that Joyce, with his highly developed auditory imagination and his unhappy estrangement from society, came to equate language and experience. We wonder whether his confidence in words was not overweening, whether he was not too articulate to achieve a really profound portrayal of human emotion. Could Joyce have apprehended the mute suffering in the eyes of the little princess, dying of childbirth in Tolstoy's *War and Peace*, or—in a different strain—the magnificent incoherence of Peeperkorn's speech, completely drowned out by the sound of a waterfall in Mann's *Der Zauberberg*? How far is language adequate to express the finer shadings and subtler modulations of the mind? 'A permanently existing "Idea" which makes its appearance before the footlights of consciousness at periodical intervals', William James tell us, 'is as mythological an entity as the Jack of Spades.' Internal monologue, for Joyce, is a way of dramatizing ideas that finds its logical climax in the external dialogue of the Circe episode. He did not bring literature any closer to life than perceptive novelists had already done; he did evolve his private mode of rhetorical discourse. He sought to illuminate the mystery of consciousness, and he ended by developing a complicated system of literary *leitmotif*.

There is nothing to prevent the internal monologue from applying to things as well as to people. Stranger voices are to be heard, and the larger cadences of city life to be rendered. Joyce feels less and less committed to the point of view of either Stephen or Bloom. Having established their respective rhythms in the morning, and brought them together at noon, he feels free to break through their soliloquies and embark upon an independent series of self-conscious stylistic adventures. The episode at the office of the *Irish Freeman*, the cave of the winds, where both heroes put in their midday appearance, is punctuated by increasingly animated headlines. Each succeeding chapter becomes more involved in style, more distorted in shape, and more permeated by what Yvor Winters considers 'the fallacy of imitative form'. Joyce meets no serious obstacles in verbalizing the atmosphere of a newspaper office, or even in finding half-chewed syllables for the sounds of Bloom's lunch: 'Table talk. I munched hum un thu Unchster Bunk un Munchday. Ha? Did you, faith?'[158] But Joyce's premise, that any given physical effect can be exactly duplicated by means of language, lures him into a confusing *mélange des genres*.

In the Siren scene, words and music are not simply associated; they are identified. Two pages, distracting and cryptic enough to have aroused the suspicions of the censorship during the last war, contain an initial statement of themes. It is easy to decode them, and to fit the fragments back into their narrative context; it is not easy to determine what song the sirens sang, or to pursue its musical pattern through the episode. When the programme notes of Joyce's commentators classify the form as *fuga per canonem*, they do not make clear whether it is the language or the situation that is being treated fugally. Should we then accept each syllable as an interval in a melodic phrase? Or should we assume that the characters work out their own counterpoint, with Bloom as subject and Boylan as counter-subject? In either case, the strict treatment of canon is unsatisfied, for there is an unlimited amount of variation. Polyphonic prose, short of the ambiguous harmonies of *Finnegans Wake*, is rarely more than a loose metaphor.

The Siren episode should not be expected to stand on its form alone, any more than any chapter in any novel. The whole passage is not a contrapuntal development of the opening phrases; the phrases are an impressionistic condensation of the passage. The introductory pages should be read as a thematic index to the following pages, but without the sequel they are meaningless. Like the lyrics in *Chamber Music*, the episode is a poem about music. The sound effects, it will be perceived, are sometimes obtained by the euphony or cacophony of words, and again—as with other objects of literary description—by the more conventional devices of quotation and reference. The banter of the barmaids and the songs of the concert room, the incessant tap of the blind man's stick and the absolute pitch of his tuning-fork, external and internal noises are duly observed and noted, sometimes by onomatopoeia and again by imagery:[242]

Bronze by gold heard the hoofirons, steelyringing

The two barmaids, Miss Lydia Douce and Miss Mina Kennedy, listen to the sound of the viceregal procession.[243]

Imperthnthn thnthnthn.

The lisping boot-boy mimics Miss Douce, when she threatens to complain of his 'impertinent insolence'.[244]

Chips, picking chips off rocky thumbnail, chips.

Mr. Dedalus strolls into the bar.[247]

Horrid! And gold flushed more.

Miss Kennedy coyly rebukes the giggling Miss Douce.[246]

A husky fifenote blew.

Mr. Dedalus takes out his pipe.[247]

Blew. Blue bloom is on the

Bloom calls for paper to write to Martha Clifford.[248]

Gold pinnacled hair.

Miss Kennedy laughs with Miss Douce, before rebuking her.[246]

A jumping rose on satiny breasts of satin, rose of Castille.

The description of the barmaids blends with Lenahan's pun: 'What opera is like a railway line?'[250]

Trilling, trilling: Idolores.

Miss Douce, polishing a tumbler, sings a song from *Floradora*.[248]

> Peep! Who's in the . . . peepofgold?

Lenahan is looking for Boylan.[248]

> Tink cried to bronze in pity.

The tink is the sound of a diner's bell. The pity is Miss Douce's. for the blind piano-tuner of whom she speaks.[249]

> And a call, pure, long and throbbing. Longindying call.

He has forgotten his tuning-fork.[250]

> Decoy. Soft word. But look! The bright stars fade. O rose! Notes chirruping answer. Castille. The morn is breaking.

Lenahan converses with the barmaid to the accompaniment of 'a voiceless song'.[250]

> Jingle jingle jaunted jingling.

Enter Boylan.[248]

> Coin rang. Clock clacked.

Boylan pays for his sloe-gin. It is almost time for his assignation.[251]

> Avowal. *Sonnze.* I could. Rebound of garter. Not leave thee. Smack. *La cloche!* Thigh smack. Avowal. Warm. Sweetheart, goodbye!

Miss Douce, to a musical background, puts on a teasing little performance for the benefit of Boylan and Lenahan.[252]

> Jingle. Bloo.

Bloom, with a sigh of relief, hears Boylan leave.[254]

> Boomed crashing chords. When love absorbs. War! War! The tympanum.

Simon Dedalus, Ben Dollard, and 'Father' Cowley gather around the piano.[256]

> A sail! A veil awave upon the waves.

Cowley sings.[257]

> Lost. Throstle fluted. All is lost now.

Stephen's uncle, Richie Goulding, lunching with Bloom, attempts to whistle an air from *La Somnambula*.[258]

> Horn. Hawhorn.

The breezy Boylan drives away in his carriage with a symbolic jeer at Bloom's impending cuckoldry.[256]

> When first he saw. Alas!

Mr. Dedalus takes over, and begins to sing an air from *Martha*: '*M'appari*'.[259]

> Full tup. Full throb.

Music and food have a mixed effect upon Bloom's emotions.[260]

> Warbling. Ah, lure! Alluring.

Bloom associates the music with his wife's singing.[261]

> Martha! Come!

The climax of the song is a guilty reminder of his own correspondence with Martha Clifford.[261]

> Clapclop. Clipclap. Clappyclap.

Applause.[262]

> Goodgod he never heard inall.

Richie Goulding reminisces about his brother-in-law's singing.[262]

> Deaf bald Pat brought pad knife took up.

The waiter brings writing materials.[264]

> A moonlit nightcall: far: far.

Mr. Dedalus attempts to recall some Italian music that he heard at Queenstown in his youth.[264]

> I feel so sad. P.S. So lonely blooming.

Bloom is answering Martha Clifford's letter.[266]

> Listen!

Miss Douce holds a sea-shell up to the ear of George Lidwell, Joyce's solicitor.[266]

> The spiked and winding cold seahorn. Have you the? Each and for other plash and silent roar.

The sound of the shell.[267]

> Pearls: when she. Liszt's rhapsodies. Hissss.

Bloom meditates on 'chamber music'.[268]

> You don't?

Miss Douce withdraws her arm from George Lidwell.[263]

> Did not: no, no: believe: Lidlyd. With a cock with a carra.

Boylan, meanwhile, is rapping at the door of 7 Eccles Street.[268]

> Black.

Cowley plays the opening chords of 'The Croppy Boy'.[268]

> Deepsounding. Do, Ben, do.

Dollard rises to sing.[268]

> Wait while you wait. Hee hee. Wait while you hee.

Bloom, in order to divert his mind from the subject of Boylan's appointment, jests desperately with himself about Pat, the waiter.[266]

> But wait!

The song is about to begin.[269]

> Low in dark middle earth. Embedded ore.

The opening chords are deep.[269]

> Naminedamine. All gone. All fallen.

The hero of the song does penance *in nomine Domini*; he is 'the last of all his race' and therefore prompts Bloom to think of himself and his dead son, Rudy.[269]

> Tiny, her tremulous fernfoils of maidenhair.

The song affects Miss Douce.[271]

> Amen! He gnashed in fury.

It reaches a climax.[272]

> Fro. To, fro. A baton cool protruding.

She manipulates the beer-pull, a symbol which synchronizes the present scene with what is happening at 7 Eccles Street.[272]

> Bronzelydia by Minagold.

Miss Douce and Miss Kennedy say farewell to a number of the company.[274]

> By bronze, by gold, in oceangreen of shadow. Bloom. Old Bloom.

Bloom, on his way out, passes by the sirens.[272]

> One rapped, one tapped with a carra, with a cock.

The sound of the cane of the blind piano-tuner, who is coming back to reclaim his tuning-fork, is answered by an echo of Boylan's crowing.[268]

> Pray for him! Pray, good people!

The song draws to a close.[272]

> His gouty fingers nakkering.

Dollard does a little Spanish dance on his way to the bar.[273]

> Big Benaben. Big Benben.

He is applauded.[273]

> Last rose Castille of summer left bloom I feel so sad alone.

Thoughts of Martha and of Lenahan's pun linger in Bloom's mind, as he goes his lonely way.[276]

> Pwee! Little wind piped wee.

He is digesting his lunch.[274]

> True men. Lid Ker Cow De and Doll. Ay, ay. Like you men. Will lift your tschink with tschunk.

Lidwell, Kernan, Cowley, Dedalus, and Dollard touch convivial glasses.[276]

> Fff! Oo!

Onomatopoeia.[276]

> Where bronze from anear? Where gold from afar? Where hoofs?

The echoes of the viceregal procession, and of the sirens, are dying out.[276]

> Rrrpr. Kraa. Kraandl.

Bloom's digestive noises are submerged in the sound of the passing tram.[276]

> Then, not till then. My eppripfftaph. Be pfrwritt.

A picture of Robert Emmet, in an antique shop outside, recalls to Bloom the last words of the dying patriot.[276]

> Done.

'When my country takes her place among the nations of the earth, then, and not till then, let my epitaph be written. I have done.'[276]

> Begin!

More and more, as the book proceeds, we are thrown back upon Joyce's talents for auditory observation. His ubiquitous ear is everywhere, and his mimicry is everybody. He is a hard-bitten hanger-on at Barney Kiernan's, gossiping of Bloom's discomfiture. He is a sentimental lady novelist, gushing over Gerty MacDowell. He is, in sudden succession, each of the principal stylists in the history of English literature. By this time, he has abandoned all pretence of adhering to the coign of vantage of certain characters. The narrative becomes clotted with Shandyan digression and inflated with sheer linguistic exuberance. The clinical small-talk of Stephen's friends, while Bloom awaits the birth of Mrs. Purefoy's child, is reported in language that recapitulates the evolution of English prose, from a primitive ritual to an American revival meeting, and that obliterates the point of the story—when Stephen gives up his key. These parodies, we are admonished, illustrate the principle of embryonic growth. We cannot take this admonition very seriously. To call in so many irrelevant authors as a middle term between the concepts of biology and the needs of the present narrative is to reduce Joyce's cult of imitative form to a final absurdity. For what organic reason, if any, must Lyly represent the foetus in the third month, and Goldsmith in the sixth? And what's Bunyan to Mrs. Purefoy, or Mrs. Purefoy to Junius?

If the *pastiche* of the hospital episode is to be justified at all, it must be considered an intrinsic part of *Ulysses*. It does offer Joyce a fair field for his technical virtuosity, and allow him again to contrast the commonplaces of today with the splendours of the past. He does embrace with gusto the opportunities for further word-play. Yet he refuses to play the truly sedulous ape. Having subverted Homer and Shakespeare to his purposes, he is not anxious to submit to the limitations of lesser writers, but rather to extend his own. When a self-effacing parodist—a Max Beerbohm —takes off a writer, the result is acute criticism. When Joyce is dealing with others, he lacks this insight and precision. His parodies reveal himself—Joyce the Jacobean divine, Joyce the Restoration diarist, Joyce the Augustan essayist, Joyce the Gothic novelist.

Here is Joyce as an Anglo-Saxon bard, no doubt the hapless Deor:[367]

> Some man that wayfaring was stood by housedoor at night's oncoming. Of Israel's folk was that man that on earth wandering far had fared. Stark ruth of man his errand that him lone led till that house.

Here is a Wardour Street approximation to the cloistered prose of Sir Thomas Malory:[373]

> But sir Leopold was passing grave maugre his word by cause he still had pity of the terrorcausing shrieking of shrill women in their labour and as he was minded of his good lady Marion that had borne him an only manchild which on his eleventh day on live had died and no man of art could save so dark is destiny.

This is a highly concentrated version of Sir Thomas Browne:[376]

> And as the ends and ultimates of all things accord in some mean and measure with their inceptions and originals, that same multiplicit concordance which leads forth growth from birth accomplishing by a retrogressive metamorphosis that minishing and ablation towards the final which is agreeable unto nature so is it with our subsolar being.

This is Joyce in a suspiciously convincing impersonation of Dickens:[402]

> And as her loving eyes behold her babe she wishes only one blessing more, to have her dear Doady there with her to share her joy, to lay in his arms that mite of God's clay, the fruit of their lawful embraces. He is older now (you and I may whisper it) and a trifle stooped in the shoulders yet in the whirligig of years a grave dignity has come to the conscientious second accountant of the Ulster bank, College Green branch.

And this is Joyce in the congenial role of Carlyle:[404]

> By heaven, Theodore Purefoy, thou has done a doughty deed and no botch! Thou art, I vow, the remarkablest progenitor barring none in this chaffering allincluding most farraginous chronicle.

Joyce's shifts from sober reality to bewildering richness, his transitions from the objective to the subjective and back—in the opinion of Sergei Eisenstein, the film director and brilliant exponent of *montage*—constitute one of the most effective applications of this technique. In the internal monologue, which Eisenstein planned to use in his unrealized production of Dreiser's *American Tragedy*, he saw a means of going beyond the literal recording of surfaces that has so exclusively preoccupied the film: 'Presenting, as it were, the play of thought within the dramatis personae—the conflict of doubts, of bursts of passion, of the voice of reason, by quick movement, or slow movement, emphasizing the difference in the rhythms of this one and that, and at the same time contrasting the almost complete absence of outward action with the feverish inward debates behind the stony mask of the face.' An unyielding naturalism, in film or fiction, must be resigned to the stalemate of total inaction. Flaubert sensed this dilemma and set aside, in *La tentation de Saint-Antoine*, a realm of symbolic action. Here the artist is still an observer, but he is also a tragic hero—a monk in the desert who might be Flaubert at Croisset or Joyce in exile. Saint Anthony is a spectator at his own tragedy, and the real actors are the sphinxes and chimeras, the fathers of the church and decadent cities of the Mediterranean, that arise in his mind.

The climax of *Ulysses*, the Circe episode, achieves its action by a similar scene of introspective drama, which Middleton Murry has compared to the *Walpurgisnacht* episode in Goethe's *Faust*. Joyce, by this time, has set going enough trains of thought and accumulated enough contexts of experience to externalize his internal dialogue before the footlights of consciousness. Just as his mock-heroics confer grandeur upon little things, so his undramatic material insists upon dramatizing itself. To turn the mind inside out, presenting its ideas and emotions as allegorical *dramatis personae*, is the procedure of the medieval morality play. It is also the programme of the expressionist movement in the modern theatre. In reaction from the naturalistic drama of Ibsen, the next generation was led by such playwrights as Strindberg in the direction of symbolism and psychic fantasy. Expressionism—as the Viennese dramatist, Hermann Bahr, defined it in 1916—sees through the eye of the mind and is active: impressionism saw through the eye of the body and was passive.

All the encounters and associations of the day—even the soap in Bloom's pocket—return for an expressionistic grand finale. In a dramatic dialogue extending through nearly a quarter of the book, to an accelerating tempo, against the backdrop of Dublin's 'nighttown', Bloom and Stephen meet. At the establishment of Bella Cohen, the sorceress who turns men into beasts, the two streams of consciousness seem to converge. It was Stephen who read in a second-hand book a charm for winning a woman's love, '*Nebrakada femininum*',[229] yet it is Bloom who hears those mystic words from his wife's apparition.[420] It was Bloom who noted at the funeral that Martin Cunningham's sympathetic face was like Shakespeare's,[88] yet it is now to Stephen that Shakespeare appears in the guise of Cunningham.[537] Both have their delusions of grandeur, as well as their anxiety-neuroses. Stephen is momentarily Cardinal Dedalus, Primate of all Ireland; Bloom is Lord Mayor, and ultimately Messiah. The incorporeal figments of both minds are strangely matched partners in a furious *danse macabre*.

There is a vulgar propriety in the musical accompaniment, Ponchielli's *Dance of the Hours*, upon which Bloom has already meditated that morning in the privy.[62] In honour of an English prostitute, Zoe,[475] there is also a *reprise* of the song played by a Scottish band that afternoon, 'My Girl's a Yorkshire Girl'.[241] Stephen is doing a *pas seul*—and tales are told of Joyce's own agility at this kind of performance—when he feels his mother's ashen breath and hears the Latin prayer he refused to say. His response is entirely in character: first an obscene monosyllable, then a phrase of expatriate French, next the echo of Lucifer's refusal, *Non serviam*, and finally a direct Wagnerian *leitmotif*, the cry of Siegfried as he wields his sword, *Nothung!* The functioning of these literary reflexes, to the dismay of Madame Cohen and her protégées, impels Stephen to action. His operatic gesture is coupled, in the stage-direction, with a reminiscence of Blake that has been on his mind since his morning class. (*He lifts his ashplant high with both hands and smashes the chandelier. Time's livid final flame leaps and, in the following darkness, ruin of all space, shattered glass and toppling masonry.*)[550]

Within a few pages, it is Bloom's turn. He is able to get Stephen out of the brothel, but not to keep him from an argument with two British privates. The argument is part reality, part hallucination; Stephen is in no condition to discriminate. Lord Tennyson in his Union Jack blazer and King Edward with his bucket are on the other side, while Stephen is backed by Bloom's Sinn Feiner and his own milkwoman, 'the old sow that eats her farrow'. The hanging of the croppy boy, last of all his race, is re-enacted for Bloom's benefit; for Stephen the black mass is celebrated. The blow that knocks him unconscious is real enough. Bloom, with the aid of the genial undertaker, Corny Kelleher, disperses the crowd, says good night to the watch, and is left alone with the prostrate figure of Stephen. It is the moment of Bloom's epiphany. Joyce, who has been at such pains to see that nothing happens all day, does not hesitate to entangle one denouement with another. Having studiously refrained from presenting any complete human relationship, he now presents the most elementary feelings on the level of psychological melodrama. With calculated bathos, Bloom is made to feel his paternity. He addresses the pitiful spectre of his son, Rudy, who died at the age of eleven days; but there is no reply—only a stage-direction:[574]

(*Gazes unseeing into Bloom's eyes and goes on reading, kissing, smiling. He has a delicate mauve face. On his suit he has diamond and ruby buttons. In his free left hand he holds a slim ivory cane with a violet bowknot. A white lambkin peeps out of his waistcoat pocket.*)

The continual effort of fiction to attain an impersonal reality seems, at first glance, to be reaching its fulfilment in *Ulysses*. Yet the more we read and reread the book, the larger it looms as a monument of personal artifice. Its scientific pretensions are sustained by the *trompe-l'œil* of literary technique. Its intellectual subtleties culminate in tried theatrical effects. This is no disparagement of Joyce, for all art is a synthesis, myth and cinema alike. If art contrives to give the illusion of reality, it is done—as they say—with mirrors, and we are concerned with how it is done. Perhaps it is because Joyce was so aware of the distinctions between art and life on the social plane, that he sought to merge them in the esthetic sphere. Perhaps he was insufficiently aware that, no matter how conscientiously experience is mirrored in literature, there will always remain something 'which into words no virtue can digest'. Bergson himself, the philosopher who held the fullest realization of the fluid nature of time and experience, also held that the intellect 'spatializes'. Consequently our imitations of life, no matter how complete and complicated we try to make them, are bound to be one-sided and over-simple.

# 3. Stasis

On the way to the burial of Paddy Dignam, Bloom shares a carriage with Simon Dedalus and several other Dubliners. Martin Cunningham tells a current anecdote about a rich money-lender, who rewarded a boatman with a florin for fishing his drowning son out of the Liffey. 'One and eightpence too much'[87] is the dry comment of Stephen's father. Stephen's mother, lately buried, is among the shades that wait at Glasnevin Cemetery. There Bloom visualizes his own infant son and his suicide father, Rudolf Virag; he remembers Mrs. Sinico—victim of 'the soul's incurable loneliness' in 'A Painful Case'—Charles Stewart Parnell, and the hosts of unremembered dead. After the ceremony, he helps the eminent solicitor, John Henry Menton, to adjust his hat, and is roundly snubbed for his pains. Good intentions and petty humiliations set the pattern of his behaviour. For one instant his unimportant life has touched history—when Parnell's hat was knocked off in a riot, and Bloom had the privilege of picking it up. After the altercation with Private Carr, he is able to do the same service for Stephen, 'history repeating itself with a difference'.[616]

All day this apologetic little man is slighted, imposed upon, and pushed around. We first meet him preparing, in all humility, his wife's breakfast. His characteristic gesture, whenever he passes other pedestrians, is to step aside. His errands are seldom successful. He is the kind of individual that street urchins follow and mimic. His shame, in the jaunty person of Blazes Boylan, seems to dog his steps. Though Bloom tries desperately to look the other way and avoid the hateful name, his internal monologue becomes agitated: 'Straw hat in sunlight. Tan shoes. Turnedup trousers. It is. It is.'[171] Bloom is seeking, and never finding, human intercourse. A stenographer, Martha Clifford, types out her lonely heart to him, but she does not see him or know his name. To a lame schoolgirl, Gerty MacDowell, he is a handsome stranger, with the saddest face she has ever seen. But, having inspired him to an act of auto-eroticism, she limps away in the twilight. The roman candles discontinue their sympathetic display, a cuckoo-clock from the house of Father Conroy—Gabriel's brother—jeers unfeelingly, and the stream of consciousness lags heavily with fatigue.

The crowning snub is administered by the next day's newspaper, which lists '*L. Boom*'[609] among Dignam's mourners. When Homer's hero concealed his name from the Cyclops, he called himself nobody, Outis. Bloom, too, is a hero in disguise, 'Everyman or Noman',[688] though he lacks all the qualifications except the disguise. He is, for Foster Damon, 'the complete misfit of all literature'. He is the apotheosis of those blighted types that Joyce sketched in *Dubliners*. He belongs to that category of mankind which Dostoevsky termed *The Insulted and the Injured*. His odyssey is the epic of psychological frustrations and social maladjustments. His climaxes are anticlimaxes. His freemasonry is an unproductive means of fellowship in Roman Catholic Dublin. His curiosity is only equalled by his gullibility. All he knows is what he reads in the papers. Interested in everything, he is thoroughly uninteresting. Self-educated and half-educated, his is the blithe optimism, the pseudo-scientific confidence, the rampant modernity of A.D. 1904. Heir of all the ages, he is a confirmed believer in —and a pathetic example of—progress. 'Make what you can of him, ye bards!'

Joyce understood that tragic stature comes neither from knowledge nor prowess, but from suffering. 'As the day wears on Bloom should overshadow them all,' he remarked to the English artist, Frank Budgen. By persecution, by adding injury to insult, he endows well-meaning mediocrity with a certain dignity. Odysseus, everywhere discomfited, everywhere resourceful, underwent his narrowest scrape in the Cave of the Cyclops. History repeats itself with a difference in Barney Kiernan's public-house. Bloom's goodwill is pitted against the Anti-Semitism of a wild Fenian shot-putter, whom Joyce denominates 'the citizen', Michael Cusack. 'A new apostle to the gentiles', sneers this redoubtable Poly-phemus. 'Universal love'.[317] Their misunderstanding is completed when the news is announced that a horse named Throwaway has won the Gold Cup. Earlier in the day, when Bloom offered Ban-tam Lyons a sporting paper, because he was 'just going to throw it away',[78] his words were taken as a tip. Now it is taken for granted that Bloom is a winner and should stand treat. Obliviously, he continues to argue about the Trinity, confounding the Father with the Son, and the Son with himself. It does not strengthen his case to bring in Spinoza and Karl Marx.

A pogrom is in sight as the Citizen hurls the biscuit box, and his mean dog, Garryowen, pursues Bloom around the corner. As we lose him in the crowd, we catch an apocalyptic glimpse of Elijah ascending to heaven in his chariot—the so-called 'second Elijah', J. Alexander Dowie, founder of Zion City, Illinois. With 'the introit in *Epiphania Domini*'[324] that accompanies this unex-pected turn of events, we realize that Joyce has had the audacity to identify his hero with Jesus Christ. His ultimate epiphany is the manifestation of God Himself, the coming of the unrecognized Messiah, whose Christian charity can only prove a source of em-barrassment in this world, can only lead him—like Jesus at the hands of Dostoevsky's Grand Inquisitor—to be crucified again. Stephen has already identified himself with Satan. His sin of pride seeks its counterpart in the virtue of love. Later, when Bloom recounts his misadventures, there is a glimmering of recognition in Stephen's mind: '*Christus* or Bloom his name is, or, after all, any other, *secundum carnem.*'[604]

For an hour in the middle of the day, the centre of gravity has shifted back from the homeless wanderer to the fatherless son, dominating a literary discussion at the National Library. 'Shake-speare is the happy hunting ground of all minds that have lost their balance,'[235] in the dictum of Haines, the obtuse Englishman who is beginning to suspect Stephen of an *idée-fixe*. The tendency to deduce Shakespeare's private life from his plays has been a favourite and rather rough sport amongst Anglo-Irish critics, from Edward Dowden to Oscar Wilde and Frank Harris. Stephen out-does them—on the impetus of three whiskies—with critical para-doxes and ingenious misquotations, as he unfolds his own theory in a vain effort to impress the lotus-eating Dublin intellectuals. Asked if he believes it, he promptly says no. The most succinct summary is his own quotation from Maeterlinck: '*If Socrates leave his house today he will find the sage seated on his doorstep.*'[201] Joyce, always finding Stephen on his own doorstep, expects Shakespeare to keep returning to Shakespeare. He expects Shake-speare, furthermore, to bear a family resemblance to Stephen. Does not his book bear the imprint of Shakespeare and Company?

'When all is said Dumas *fils* (or is it Dumas *père*?) is right,' declares John Eglinton, with meaningful equivocation. 'After God Shakespeare has created most.'[201] Shakespeare is the supreme artificer, the paternal spirit of Dædalus, forging the uncreated consciousness of mankind. *Hamlet* and his problems inevitably become an 'objective correlative', in T. S. Eliot's phrase, for the problems of the artist. For Hamlet, as for Telemachus and Stephen and Joyce, there are usurpers in his father's house. The rock of Scylla is the familiar and philistine world of Stratford or Dublin. The whirlpool of Charybdis is the sea of troubles that overwhelms the exile in London or Paris. Stephen hears 'the note of banishment, banishment from the heart, banishment from home',[200] sounding uninterruptedly in Shakespeare's creations. 'It's quite simple,' Mulligan has explained to Haines. 'He proves by algebra that Hamlet's grandson is Shakespeare's grandfather and that he himself is the ghost of his own father.'[16]

That is possibly an oversimplification. He does confound him-self with Hamlet, and Shakespeare with the role he actually played, the ghost of Hamlet's father. He also confounds Hamlet with Shakespeare's own son, Hamnet. He interprets Anne Hathaway, at home in Stratford, as a faithless Penelope—and Shakespeare, homesick in London, as a cuckold. He is challenged to prove Shakespeare a Jew, and unhesitatingly responds by expounding the Thomist definition of incest, an avarice of the emotions: 'He means that the love so given to one near in blood is covetously withheld from some stranger who, it may be, hungers for it. Jews, whom Christians tax with avarice, are of all races the most given to intermarriage.'[194] Bloom, by implication, is a worthier object of Stephen's filial love than Simon Dedalus. Fatherhood is 'a mystical estate, an apostolic succession, from only begetter to only begotten . . . *Amor matris*, subjective and objective genitive, may be the only true thing in life. Paternity may be a legal fiction.'[195] And Stephen's obsession carries him off to the clouds of theology, to the controversial dogma of the *filioque* and the subtle heresy of Sabellius, the consubstantiality of Father and Son.

Bloom, unnoticed during this exhibition, has slipped in and out of the library to look up an advertisement. The single vague fragment of poetry which he could summon to mind in the previous hour happened to be a line of Shakespeare, '*Hamlet, I am thy father's spirit*.'[141] His wanderings have already crossed the aimless path of his incognizant godson, on the way to Glasnevin Cemetery and in the office of the *Irish Freeman*. In the afternoon both pause in the same book-shop, and in the evening they come together at the hospital. When Stephen leaves for 'nighttown' with a drunken party of medical students, Bloom follows. They catch up with each other at Bella Cohen's. 'Jewgreek is greekjew. Extremes meet,'[479] announces Lynch's cap, a minor character in the macabre fantasy of the Circe episode. The importance of all kinds of hats in Bloom's *modus vivendi*—from Parnell to Martha Clifford —is only another aspect of Joyce's procedure for making the most of the simplest commodities and slightest coincidences. We have only to glance back at Fielding's chapter on hats in *Jonathan Wild* to conclude that heroic irony, with Joyce, has softened and taken on a sentimental tinge.

In the small hours of June 17th Bloom and Stephen can finally begin their conversation. The hut of the swineherd, Eumæus, is an open-all-night shebeen presided over by a Dublin character, Skin-the-Goat, whose claim to notoriety was a suspected complicity in the Phoenix Park murders. There, perforce, they must listen to the tall talk of a red-bearded sailor, W. B. Murphy, who has come ashore at eleven o'clock in the morning from the *Rosevean*,[587] the three-master which made its first appearance on the horizon at the end of Stephen's walk.[47] We can chart the course of this ship, as it enters the harbour and unloads its cargo in the afternoon,[236] by the crumpled handbill—an announcement of the coming of 'Elijah' Dowie—which Bloom has dropped into the Liffey as he crossed the bridge in the forenoon.[141] By means of these mechanical contrivances, the book achieves an organic quality. When we view life collectively, Joyce would suggest, we see how men are related to things. Nothing is irrelevant. Everything moves in its appointed orbit. The most ill-assorted phenomena are equally parts of an all-encompassing whole.

When we view life individually, we see how men are related to men, usually—in Joyce—through the indirect means of things. What, within that vast and complex organism, is the relation between two given human beings? What, in other words, can Stephen and Bloom have to say to each other? Stephen, having no place to go, is glad to accompany Bloom. Bloom, on the walk home, enjoys giving Stephen a word of fatherly warning against his friends, particularly Mulligan. He likes to believe, as he does the honours of 7 Eccles Street, that the scientific and artistic temperaments are facing each other across his kitchen table. The dialogue between popular science and tired Thomism is unrelievedly painful and banal. Their musical tastes differ drastically: Bloom prefers the grand opera of the Jewish composer Meyerbeer, Stephen the Elizabethan airs of John Dowland, who dwelt in the suburb of Dalkley where Joyce's family lived. Bloom repeats a few faltering phrases in Hebrew, Stephen in Gaelic. With every futile question and perfunctory reply, they become more aware of the barriers that separate them—name and age, race and creed. Granted two men living in Dublin, dissatisfied and disinherited, they share a pitiful minimum of common ground.[627]

Did Bloom discover common factors of similarity between their respective like and unlike reactions to experience?

Both were sensitive to artistic impressions musical in preference to plastic or pictorial. Both preferred a continental to an insular manner of life, a cisatlantic to a transatlantic place of residence. Both indurated by early domestic training and an inherited tenacity of heterodox resistance professed their disbelief in many orthodox religious, national, social and ethical doctrines. Both admitted the alternately stimulating and obtunding influence of heterosexual magnetism.

There is no leeway for nostalgia in the description of Bloom's homecoming. By suddenly shifting from the subjective to the objective, by pursuing the form of a catechism to its logical conclusion, Joyce reaches the dead end of naturalistic detachment. Instead of emotions, he records statistics about the Dublin water-supply; instead of sensations, data about the conductivity of heat along a spoon; instead of communication, a mathematical computation of respective ages. Bloom is thirty-eight, Stephen twenty-two. Their lives are related only by the widest generalities or the most extraneous details. A third isolated existence has casually touched their own: Mrs. Riordan, who took care of Stephen when he was a child, lived in the same hotel with Bloom, shortly after he was married and shortly before she died. Neither is conscious of an even more casual connection: Simon Dedalus—interloper in the household of Odysseus—may have been one of the lovers of Molly Bloom. Bloom's daughter, Milly, who is taking after her mother, turns out to be the friend of a medical friend of Stephen's, Alec Bannon. The world is smaller than either Stephen or Bloom is willing to concede at this point.

At this point, as Stephen declines Bloom's further hospitality and shakes his hand in farewell, the world becomes infinitesimally small. One-thirty is sounded by the bells of the nearby Saint George's church, [665] with the same weary *Heigho* that Bloom heard at eight-forty-five in the morning,[62] and that has been tolling the death of Dignam in his thoughts through the interim.[449] For Stephen the same bells sound another echo, the last echo of his internal monologue, the last we hear of him: '*Liliata rutilantium. Turma circumdet.*' It was in Eccles Street, we remember, that he experienced his first epiphany, before a house which seemed 'the very incarnation of Irish paralysis'. We turn back to take our leave of Bloom, reduced to the most abject dimensions by a glance into

the future, 'the aged impotent disfranchised ratesupported moribund lunatic pauper'.[686] We comprehend at last the word that has
been puzzling him for so long, 'parallax', the allowance which
astronomers make for a displaced angle of observation.

Surely Mr. Gorman, when he states that the mood of the
Penelope episode was influenced by an astronomical film, must be
thinking of this chapter, the Ithaca episode. Here, if anywhere,
Joyce contemplates his characters *sub specie aeternitatis*, from the
scope of planetary distances. The echoes for the moment have
died away, and we shudder, like Pascal, before the eternal silence
of infinite spaces. We have come all the way with Stephen Dedalus,
from the Class of Elements to the Universe. The receding view of
snow over Ireland that we took at the end of *Dubliners* is now our
bleak perspective for the world itself. Nature displays the same
ironic indifference, the same remote and stony unconcern with
man, that is so spectacularly exhibited in the epilogue to Hardy's
*Dynasts*, where the map of Europe shrinks to a prostrate human
body, and the diminished sphere goes whirling off to be lost
among the other stars.

The cosmic background and the domestic foreground, in spite
of incongruities of scale, exist on the same plane. They form a
meticulously amplified stage setting, in the manner of Ibsen
pushed to microscopic and telescopic extremes. The most explicit
documentation of the book is brought to bear upon Bloom's
shabby house and petty-bourgeois chattels: the nondescript library
that catalogues his mind, the matter-of-fact budget that itemizes
his day, the miscellaneous contents of his desk, including the
suicide note of Rudolf Virag. The dense material element with
which Joyce surrounds his '*Favourite Hero*'[646] is all too familiar,
*mutatis mutandis*, to American readers. Bloom and his many
devices—his Sandow exerciser, his patent wonder-worker, the
gadgets he is always inventing, his schemes to get rich quick, his
ambition to own a model home in a garden suburb, his vision of a
vaguely socialistic régime of universal brotherhood—might be the
subject of a Walt Whitman panegyric in an unprecedentedly minor
key, or a Sinclair Lewis satire of unaccustomed insight and warmth.

Bloom is neither, or rather both, for Joyce treats the subject of the common man with his dual formula of irony and pathos. Ironic pathos attains its climax in the maudlin apparition of Rudy. Bloom's emotion is clothed in sentimentality, but this very sentimentality provokes our emotion. The more we understand the forces which frustrate them, the more we sympathize with his frustrated impulses. Pathetic irony, on the other hand, can scarcely be carried beyond the point at which we leave him. By a typographical oddity, inadvertently left out of English and American editions of *Ulysses*, Bloom's internal monologue comes to a full stop with a large dot. With this exact locus in time and space, with the latitude and longitude of himself and his wife in their profaned bed, consciousness darkens. Bloom's final page harks back to Stephen's awakening page, at the beginning of the *Portrait of the Artist*, and looks forward to the drowsy pages of *Finnegans Wake*. Simultaneously, he is the fabulous hero, home from his wanderings, and the 'childman weary, the manchild in the womb'.[697]

Womb? Weary?
He rests. He has travelled.

With?
Sinbad the Sailor and Tinbad the Tailor and Jinbad the Jailer and Whinbad the Whaler and Ninbad the Nailer and Finbad the Failer and Binbad the Bailer and Pinbad the Pailer and Minbad the Mailer and Hinbad the Hailer and Rinbad the Railer and Dinbad the Kailer and Vinbad the Quailer and Linbad the Yailer and Xinbad the Phthailer.

When?
Going to dark bed there was a square round Sinbad the Sailor roc's auk's egg in the night of the bed of all the auks of the rocs of Darkinbad the Brightdayler.

Where?

After Stephen has withdrawn and Bloom has retired, Joyce dismisses the problems of the artist, the adjustments of the city, and the ephemeral worries of men. He gives up the negations and contradictions of the day and embraces the changeless and changing renewal of night. The book has turned gradually away from history and back to nature. The concluding episode, like the last distich of *Faust*, attaches its hopes to the eternal feminine: '*Das Ewig-Weibliche zieht uns hinan.*' Joyce's heroine does not lead us in so spiritualized a direction as Goethe's, but her nocturnal ruminations do lead us through forty-five unpunctuated pages before she falls asleep. The course of these meanderings is pervaded by the monthly rhythms of female nature. In the recumbent 'attitude of Gea-Tellus',[697] she incarnates the fertility of earth. She is the compliant body as Stephen is the uncompromising mind, and as Bloom—torn between them—is the lacerated heart. To Stephen's everlasting nay, she opposes a final affirmation.

Molly Bloom, at thirty-three, is in the ripe possession of physical charms inherited from her mother, a Spanish Jewess. The name of her father, an Irish officer stationed at Gibraltar, Major Tweedy, is all that is left of Penelope's weaving. With animal placidity, she can refer to the corselet which she knitted for Rudy's burial, and which has figured so tenderly in her husband's thoughts as 'that woollen thing'.[700] During the ten years since their child's death, they have become physically and mentally estranged. Their conjugal relationship is the merest cohabitation. The cold statistics of the previous chapter imply that twenty-five others might have shared her favours with Bloom.[692] From her latest lover, Boylan, she is undergoing a revulsion, as the afternoon passes through her mind in remorseless review. Toward Stephen, piqued by her husband's narrative, her thoughts now stray. Her attitude toward him, toward Bloom, toward all men is largely maternal—the attitude of a woman who has lost an only son. To Ulysses she is faithful in her fashion—the fashion of Chaucer's Wife of Bath or Defoe's *Moll Flanders*, though she disapproves of the latter.[716]

Her internal monologue is no closer to life, and no less literary than the prologue of the former. 'It didn't make me blush,' Molly confesses of a bawdy song, 'why should it either its only nature.'[736] Yet she protests altogether too much. All of Joyce's characters have something of his own preoccupation with language. Molly uses certain elementary monosyllables without inhibition, but with a self-conscious realization that they have never been printed in a work of serious fiction before. They rarely sound natural, and never look natural, for few readers are likely to have seen them outside of the *graffiti* of public lavatories. They could not, as a matter of literary convention, be simply and spontaneously introduced, and the feelings which they denote would never need to be verbalized so deliberately. Joyce has faced the difficulties of putting such things into words, and of putting such words into books, but it cannot be said that he has surmounted them. It can only be said that he has come a long way from the second chapter of the *Portrait of the Artist*, where he substituted a purple passage for an obscene scrawl.

Mr. Gorman speaks of an Italian letter suggesting the Penelope episode, though he discreetly refrains from mentioning how this literary source fell into Joyce's hands. It is rash, of course, to assume that a man can penetrate the stream of consciousness of a woman. Dorothy Richardson has written a whole series of novels on the contrary assumption: that no masculine novelist has ever understood the feminine mentality. It may be merely a rash assumption that the internal monologue can ever be anything but an inside job: Proust never attempted to apply the method to other characters than himself, and Virginia Woolf's attempts are not so successful as her self-portraits. Neither Leopold nor Molly Bloom could ever be as real to Joyce, and therefore to us, as Stephen Dedalus. His monologue, literary and introspective as Joyce himself, is more psychologically valid than theirs. They are both passive characters, receptacles for impressions—of city life with Bloom, of sexual experience with Molly. Molly's more specialized range makes her a monolithic symbol, the massive goddess of some primitive rite. Her last word, blended with her memories of first love at Gibraltar and first surrender to Bloom, repeats itself until it becomes an incantation of assent to the fundamental act of the race:[742]

O that awful deepdown torrent O and the sea the sea crimson sometimes like fire and the glorious sunsets and the figtrees in the Alameda gardens yes and all the queer little streets and pink and blue and yellow houses and the rosegardens and the jessamine and geraniums and cactuses and Gibraltar as a girl where I was a Flower of the mountain yes when I put the rose in my hair like the Andalusian girls used or shall I wear a red yes and how he kissed me under the Moorish wall and I thought well as well him as another and then I asked him with my eyes to ask again yes and then he asked me would I yes to say yes my mountain flower and first I put my arms around him yes and drew him down to me so he could feel my breasts all perfume yes and his heart was going like mad and yes I said yes I will Yes.

In a distinguished critical essay, Opinion A. 110-59 of the United States District Court, Southern District of New York, rendered 6th December 1933, Judge John M. Woolsey considers the novelty of Joyce's methods, the sincerity of his intentions, the legal definition of pornography, and the right of *Ulysses* to be admitted into the United States. 'But my considered opinion, after long reflection', he concludes, 'is that whilst in many places the effect of "Ulysses" on the reader undoubtedly is somewhat emetic, nowhere does it tend to be an aphrodisiac.' It is noteworthy that, in vindicating the book from the charge of obscenity, Judge Woolsey should describe its effect in terms of catharsis, the purge of the emotions through pity and terror that Aristotle attributes to tragedy. 'Aristotle has not defined pity and terror. I have,' Stephen pontificated, in the *Portrait of the Artist*. 'Pity is the feeling which arrests the mind in the presence of whatsoever is grave and constant in human sufferings and unites it with the human sufferer.'[232] Terror, on the other hand, 'unites it with the secret cause'. With Bloom we feel a sense of terror before the pressures that have shaped him. With Stephen we feel a sense of pity, to the extent that we accept his ideals.

He has sharply distinguished the esthetic emotions from the improper arts, pornographic or didactic. 'You see I use the word *arrest*. I mean that the tragic emotion is static. . . . The feelings excited by improper art are kinetic. . . .'[233] The proper state of mind to be awakened by beauty, according to Stephen, is a standstill, 'an esthetic stasis'. This requires three qualities, in the words he has translated from Aquinas: *'wholeness, harmony and radiance'*.[241]

How can *Ulysses*, by these criteria, be a thing of beauty? The immediate qualities which make it so poignant an expression of the modern mind, for most readers, are chaos, dissonance, and obscurity. The paradox of the book is that it imposes a static ideal upon kinetic material. The esthetic problem is to work out an arrangement for disorder. The social issue is to balance an unstable equilibrium. The theme of the city calls for particular and perpetual movement. The pattern of the artist makes for universal and timeless repose.

The mere phrase, 'motion picture', promises a way out of this impasse. We are quite aware that the optical illusion of reality may be obtained from a continuity of discrete shots, and we have found reasons for comparing the composition of *Ulysses* to the *montage* of films. We should be misled by a metaphor, however, if we were not ready to grant that Joyce's medium is far less vivid and swift, far more blurred and jerky. His projections, to our surprise, tend to slow down and at times to stop altogether, suddenly arresting the action and suspending the characters in mid-air. Such are the obstacles of adapting the screen to the novel. Action is impeded by the accumulation of details, and characters are inhibited by the limits of their stock responses. But Joyce, even in the heat of practical experiments, remains true to his classical theories. His sense of movement is all on the surface. His underlying purpose is to call a halt, to achieve a stasis, to set up an immovable object against the irresistible forces of the city.

The central episode of the Wandering Rocks is a scale model of *Ulysses*, as the book is a scale model of the city. It starts with Father Conmee, taking a walk after lunch, and is brought to a close by the Earl of Dudley, taking a ride in his carriage. The streets are crowded with Dubliners, whose greetings are now and then acknowledged by the Jesuit rector or the British Viceroy. A one-legged sailor, the blind piano-tuner, the five sandwich-men, other pedestrians and other vehicles cross and pass and keep moving. Bloom quits the bookstall before Stephen enters; and Stephen, though he finds his own sister there, feels only isolation. In great cities men are brought together by a desire of gain,' in

Disraeli's analysis. 'They are not in a state of co-operation, but of isolation.' The gregarious bustle goes on as a matter of routine. Streets intersect, shops advertise, homes have party walls, and fellow citizens depend upon the same water-supply; but there is no co-operation between human beings. The individual stands motionless, like Odysseus becalmed by the doldrums:[138]

At various points along the eight lines tramcars with motionless trolleys stood in their tracks, bound for or from Rathmines, Rathfarnham, Blackrock, Kingstown and Dalkey, Sandymount Green, Ringsend and Sandymount Tower, Donnybrook, Palmerston Park and Upper Rathmines, all still, becalmed in short circuit. Hackney cars, cabs, delivery waggons, mailvans, private broughams, aerated mineral water floats with rattling crates of bottles, rattled, rolled, horsedrawn, rapidly.

*Ulysses* is totally lacking in the epic virtues of love, friendship, and magnanimity. Ulysses and Telemachus have broken bread and washed together, and Ulysses and Penelope have gone to bed together; but there is no communication between father and son, no intercourse between husband and wife. 'From the description of the meeting between Ulysses and Telemachus it is plain that Homer considered it quite as dreadful for relations who had long been separated to come together again as for them to separate in the first instance. And that is about true,' asserted an unorthodox Homeric scholar and inveterate father-hater, Samuel Butler. Some of Joyce's commentators, it is true, discern a subtle change in the lives of his characters, and applaud a subdued drama in the events of June 16th. Joyce in his determination to stick to the schedule, gives them no grounds to hope for any reunion. His consistent aim would be thwarted if there were real motion in his final picture. Bloom and Stephen would lose half their poignance if they had any reprieve from the soul's incurable loneliness.

Molly, to be sure, will comfort the wanderer by getting his breakfast on June 17th. Nothing, however, will come of Stephen's Italian lessons, to which she and her husband, in their different ways, have already begun to look forward. She has always accepted, with her own reservations, the timid fetishism of Bloom's devotion, and her role will continue to be that of tolerant acceptance on her own terms. Tomorrow will be another day and, for Bloom, a similar Odyssey. He will set out again and travel over his restless course, until—like Dante's Ulisse—he ventures beyond the Pillars of Hercules and is wrecked in a whirlwind before the island Mount of Purgatory. Further wanderings can only bring further sufferings. Stephen has made up his mind to put the tower and the school behind him, and to go into second exile. He will never forget the day because it has strengthened his decision. No one seems to have been amused by the *Pisgah Sight of Palestine*, his parable of two old crones who climb to the top of Nelson's Pillar with a sack of plums, and spit out the stones upon the city below. 'Ten years,' Mulligan scoffs to Haines, who is an enthusiast for Irish culture. 'He is going to write something in ten years.'[236]

In ten years Joyce is going to complete the *Portrait of the Artist* and undertake *Ulysses*. The rest of his life, whatever the place of exile, is a ceaseless endeavour to recapture his own past. With the cunning of the artificer, the patience of the archaeologist, and the mixed emotions of the expatriate, he constructs a replica of Dublin on the day when time stood still. He exalts the labours of artifice into an act of creation, and thus he comes to regard the artist as a demiurge. Only by playing god can he settle his own predicament —the predicament of the son dispossessed by his environment, and of the artist who can never possess his subject. But he cannot penetrate, any more than Yeats or any other, 'the labyrinth of another's being'. He can mediate between himself and a fellow citizen, but he cannot assume the duties of citizenship. His fellow citizen, Mr. Bloom, is the sorrier exile. A mute inglorious Shakespeare, a rejected Messiah, he has nothing to offer Stephen but a pathetic object-lesson. Something is lacking from the lives of both, and all of Bloom's advertising enterprise will not supply the deficiency:[67]

> *What is home without*
> *Plumtree's Potted Meat?*
> *Incomplete.*
> *With it an abode of bliss.*

Both are at sea, helpless among the cross-currents of contemporary life, the common man drifting from shabby ambition to dismal frustration, the artist obsessed with the intricacies of his own personality and his special craft. Joyce's work commemorates the long-standing quarrel between the bourgeois and the bohemian. The art of a society which has had little use for art, it expresses that society by way of protest. Joyce seeks a guide in Homer and a father in Shakespeare. Yet his favourite philosopher, Vico, was the first to maintain that Homer had been many poets, a collective expression of Hellenic life. And Stephen's own arguments reveal—if anything—how thoroughly Shakespeare's individuality has been submerged in the homogeneous and high-spirited culture of the Elizabethan age. The figure of the artist towers over the model of Dublin, in *Ulysses*, and that is why Joyce's conception of a personal epic is a contradiction in terms. A singleness of purpose and a breadth of treatment, almost unparalleled in literature, have done their utmost to bring about the synthesis. 'If there is any difficulty in what I write it is because of the material I use,' he once remarked. 'The thought is always simple.' The material is continually fluctuating with the speed of cinema. The thought is constantly aspiring toward the permanence of myth.

'To some of Joyce's younger contemporaries, like myself,' T. S. Eliot wrote recently, in a letter which the London *Times* refused to print, '*Ulysses* still seems the most considerable work of imagination in English in our time, comparable in importance (though in little else) with the work of Marcel Proust.' In distinguishing Joyce from the novelist with whom he is most often compared, Mr. Eliot shows his customary acumen. Proust's *esprit de finesse* is the very reverse of Joyce's *esprit de géométrie*. In *A la recherche du temps perdu* the thought is frequently complex, but the material is relatively simple: through a rambling series of lyrical essays and dramatic scenes, Proust conveys his profound sense of the growth and change of character. His mind is temporal, while Joyce's is spatial. Characterization in Joyce is finally reducible to a few stylized gestures and simplified attitudes. His characters move in space, but they do not develop in time. They only look forward to the ruin of all space, to time's livid final flame, to doomsday. *Ulysses* is not so rich in psychological insight as in technical brilliance. The burning intensity of Joyce's own creative effort animates the statuesque coldness of his creations. It beats down, like an aroused volcano upon an ancient city, overtaking the doomed inhabitants in forum or temple, at home or at brothel, and petrifying them in the insensate agonies of paralysis.

# III

---

*The Fabulous Artificer*

# 1. The Nightmare of History

*Ulysses* stood for seventeen years as the last word in both symbolism and naturalism. It was attacked and defended, imitated and diluted, pirated and bowdlerized, taken for granted and reacted from, but never eclipsed in the richness of its technique or the reality of its material. A generation of critics lived in its shadows, terrified at the prospect of a sequel, and secretly convinced that anything short of the millennium would be an anticlimax. *Work in Progress* did little to allay these terrors, for *Finnegans Wake*—though it replaces the archangel's trumpet with an electric amplifier, and relies upon the news agencies of this world—was to be Joyce's unique last judgement and genial proclamation of doom. 'Calling all downs. Calling all downs to dayne. Array! Surrection. Eireweeker to the wohld bludyn world. O rally, O rally, O rally! Phlenxty, O rally! . . . Tass, Patt, Staff, Woff, Havv, Bluvv, and Rutter. The smog is lofting. . . . Sonne feine, somme feehn avaunt! Guld modning, have yous viewsed Piers' aube? . . . The leader, the leader!'[593]

A millennium must be expected to produce confusion, to require and reward patience. In Joyce's last book, as—we take it—on the last day, too much is happening at once to yield any single impression. Different witnesses have deposed contradictory testimony. Our attempts to criticize *Finnegans Wake*, in the two years since its definitive appearance, have been about as accurate and as adequate as the efforts of Æsop's blind men to describe an elephant. Lacking the full perspective that Joyce alone had eyes to see, we have been left with one of the white elephants of literature. The reader to whom it is addressed, 'that ideal reader suffering from an ideal insomnia',[120] was the author. Since no one else can be trusted to unravel his fullest implications or construe his ultra-violet allusions or improvise his lost chords, everyone else is relieved of responsibility. If we cannot fathom the depths of the book, we can enjoy its surfaces. If it withholds its innermost secrets from us, it is lavish with small souvenirs. In spite of its publicized privacy, there is something for everyone in *Finnegans Wake*. It is, in Joyce's happy coinage, a *funferal*.

The stream of unconsciousness in *Finnegans Wake* begins at the very point where the stream of consciousness in *Ulysses* left off—the point of falling asleep. For the last time we return to Dublin, where we spent an exhaustive day with Mr. Bloom, to enjoy an exhausting night with Mr. Earwicker. All of his adventures, like those of Bloom and Stephen under the spell of Circe, take place in the twilight regions of psychic fantasy. His revelation, like Scipio's or Dante's, Scrooge's or Alice's, is not less significant because it is only a dream. The dream vision, that favourite form of medieval allegory, is the shaping conception of 'this nonday diary, this all-nights newseryreel',[489] and poetic archaisms like 'methought' and 'meseemed' are in character.[403] Since Chaucer brought to life the conventions of the *Roman de la rose*, realism in fiction has come full circle. To our contemporaries, turning back from the sophisticated toward the primitive, Freud has indicated and Kafka has exemplified the connection between myths and dreams. Sleep, the most intimate of experiences, is also the most universal. Through Joyce's private investigations of the mind, we return to the public domain of myth.

'To write a dream which shall resemble the real course of a dream, with all its inconsistency, its strange transformations, which are all taken as a matter of course, its eccentricities and aimlessness —with nevertheless a leading idea running through the whole. Up to this old age of the world, no such thing ever has been written.' Our older and sadder and wiser age, in realizing this project of Nathaniel Hawthorne's, compresses its accumulated sense of the past into the haphazard dream-work. The nightmare from which Joyce was trying to awake is history. It moves toward one great goal, Mr. Deasy told Stephen, the manifestation of God. But

Stephen's definition of God is 'a shout in the street', and the apotheosis of *Ulysses* is the clamour that hounds Bloom out of the public-house. Our final impression of the *Portrait of the Artist* is the sound of hoofs on the road in the heavy night, 'through the silence of the city which has turned from dreams to dreamless sleep.' The course of history, in Joyce's dream-like rendering, is orchestrated to the street cries and nocturnal noises of Dublin. Events finally dwindle away, and nothing remains except echoes: the recently published *Pastimes of James Joyce* offer a posthumous salute to President Roosevelt under the honorific title of 'the big noise'.

Street life and Homeric legend are scrupulously differentiated throughout *Ulysses*. The locus for *Finnegans Wake* is that point in infinity where such parallels meet. Earwicker's larder is stocked with wholesome Roman orators like 'Burrus' and 'Caseous',[161] while his wife's dressing-table is consecrated to such inverted Egyptian deities as 'Enel-Rah' and 'Aruc-Ituc'.[237] Out of the small-beer chronicle of this nondescript household, clouded by the phantasmagoria of 'a trying thirstay mournin',[6] emanate not one but many myths. To integrate them, we need not a classical epic but a universal history. We desert Homer for the Neapolitan polymath of the eighteenth century who raised the so-called Homeric question. 'The producer (Mr. John Baptister Vickar)'[255] is better known as the philosopher, Giambattista Vico. It was he who first claimed that the *Iliad* and the *Odyssey* were not the successive products of the prime and age of a single poetic personality, but the continuous autobiography of the Greek people. In the mythologies of poets, he discovered a symbolic record of prehistory. In the etymologies of words, he discerned the lost wisdom of the ancients. A rhetorician as well as a historian, he shared Joyce's two-fold preoccupation with language and myth.

Vico's *Scienza Nuova* is an ambitious and obscure treatise, combining a rather tame philosophical eclecticism with an exceptionally keen historiographic insight. For the first hundred years of its existence, it was almost totally ignored. During the past century it has been resurrected to serve the various ends of Michelet, Croce, and Joyce. A philosophy which has room for such bedfellows could only exist in the limbo between mysticism and empiricism, between traditional and modern thought. Joyce was especially devoted to certain anti-scholastic thinkers who stray along the outskirts of the Catholic tradition. In *Finnegans Wake* we encounter *passim* the wayward spectre of Nicholas of Cusa. At every turn we stumble over a quarrelsome pair, who sometimes go about representing a Dublin firm of booksellers, Messrs. Browne & Nolan, but more often reincarnate the perturbed spirit of Giordano Bruno and his birthplace in southern Italy, Nola. It was 'the Nolan', we recollect, who sponsored Joyce's first pamphlet, 'The Day of the Rabblement', and who abetted Stephen's undergraduate heresy in the *Portrait of the Artist*. It was the same Bruno who likened his own martyrdom to that of Icarus, *'del figliuòlo di Dedalo il fin rio'*, and who attributed his whole system of metaphysics to the efficient cause of an internal artificer, *artefice interno*.

The Brunonian doctrine which commends itself to Joyce is an aggressive reconciliation of the antitheses of the schoolmen. Since form and matter are father and mother, the Adam and Eve of Bruno's pantheistic universe, all created things are the unruly offspring of the demiurge of intellect and the matrix of necessity. *Finnegans Wake* spins a giddy commentary on this doctrine.[488] *Ulysses* had avowed that the conflicting interests of artist and citizen were irreconcilable. The later work exaggerates this avowal by suspiciously regarding all men as potential antagonists, and by ruthlessly dichotomizing its *dramatis personae*. In the theological sphere the conflict is waged between 'Mick' and 'Nick', the Archangel Michael and the devil. All the battles of history are summed up in the antagonism of Napoleon and the Duke of Wellington, and cheerfully rehearsed during a visit to the 'museyroom'.[8] Joyce sees eternal opposites, as Sir Thomas Browne saw quincunxes, everywhere—Cain and Abel, Castor and Pollux, Guelf and Ghibelline, York and Lancaster, Stella and Vanessa, the 'Mookse' and the 'Gripes', the 'Ondt' and 'Gracehoper', and, last but not least, the 'musichall pair', Shem and Shaun.[408]

Sooner or later these dichotomies 'by the coincidance of their contraries reamalgamerge', with the endless plasticity of Ovid's

*Metamorphoses* and the daft ingenuity of Walt Disney's *Silly Symphonies*. Nicholas of Cusa, for one, allies himself to Bloom's old enemy in 'Micholas de Cusack'.[49] Joyce's book not only clothes Bruno's abstractions in motley, but actually bears out Vico's theories. The most far-reaching of these can be stated in three words: history repeats itself. It is, in Joyce's phrase, 'a theory none too rectiline of the evolution of human society and a testament of the rocks from all the dead unto some the living'.[73] The pattern of repetition, as established by Vico and followed by Joyce, is a historical version of Dante's eschatology: *Inferno, Purgatorio, Paradiso*. Three consecutive periods are characterized as divine, heroic, and civil. Each period contributes its characteristic institution (religion, marriage, and burial rites) and its corresponding virtue (piety, honour, and duty). The inarticulate dark ages give way to the fabulous, and then the historical, forms of literary expression; the original hieroglyphic language is succeeded by metaphorical speech, and at length by an epistolary style and a profane vernacular. The rise of cities is the sum of three epochs of man's activity, yet the ruins of bygone civilization foreshadow the fall of cities.

The fourth epoch and the peculiar twist in Vico's philosophy of history, is the cyclic movement by which the third period swings back into the first again *da capo*. That it does so is a thesis which few of Joyce's contemporaries are disposed to deny. They may take what consolation they can from Vico's bland belief that the cycles continue to spiral upwards and onwards. A long-range optimism is reflected in the provisional title, *Work in Progress*. Mankind, viewed under the aspect of eternity, is 'a human pest cycling (pist!) and recycling (past!)'.[99] A composite picture of this active individual would be somewhat blurred, but into it might be concentrated the entire development of human awareness. That, at any rate, is what Joyce undertakes to perform with his time machine, his 'wholemole millwheeling vicociclometer'.[614] His hero 'moves in vicous cicles'.[134] Vico himself, by a process of naturalization typical of Joyce, is brought back to Ireland to become an eponymous hero of the rocky road to Dublin, of a street in Dalkey previously mentioned during the history lesson in *Ulysses*.[246] 'The Vico road goes round and round to meet where terms begin.'[452]

To simplify the complications of life, Joyce has Vico's precedent for treating nations as families and breaking down society into a small number of recurrent types (or 'tips'). The plot is little more than a series of verbal associations and numerical correspondences. Relationships are often clearer than significances. Numerology is a method of characterization,[13] and every character has his number.[486] The *ingénue* has twenty-eight understudies because, like Frederick in *The Pirates of Penzance*, she seems to have been born on the last day of February in a leap year.[147] A street number masquerading as a date, 1132, is both the address of a misplaced letter[420] and an entry in the annals of the Middle Ages: the accession of Saint Malachy to the primacy of the Irish church, eighteen years after Brian Boru routed the Danes at the battle of Clontarf.[473] The temporal numbers twelve and four, in particular, seem invested with all the mystical meaning that Dante reserved for the number three. The year has twelve months, the night twelve hours. We hear the bells of twelve churches; we try vainly to make out whether the twelve members of the jury we must face are the twelve customers with whom we got drunk in the pub last night. The four walls of the bedroom speak with the voices of the four evangelists, who are the spokesmen of the four provinces of Ireland. Matt Gregory, Marcus Lyons, Luke Tarpey, and the laggard Ulsterman, Johnny MacDougall, are the Four Masters, legendary chroniclers of their country's legends.[91] The four sections of *Finnegans Wake* approximate Vico's periods of civilization, which recapitulate the four seasons of the year and the four ages of men, 'from tomittot to teetootomtotalitarian'.[260]

The first section, 'only a fadograph of a yestern scene',[7] reproduces the most primitive phase, citing the anthropological authority of Professor Lévy-Bruhl.[150] Against a prehistoric landscape swarming with the 'brontoichthyan' forms of 'oystrygods gaggin fishygods', and a horizon dotted with cromlechs and menhirs, a race of giants and cyclops bestrides the land.[4] 'Astoneaged',[18] we begin to pick up floating debris of biblical lore and old wives' tales of tribal heroes—Caractacus,[48] Ragnar,[64] Vercingetorix,[66] Roland and his horn.[74] Now, according to Vico, the function of prime mover in this chaotic state of affairs is performed by the thunder, which inspires men with fear and hence religion: the name they accord it is their name for God. In retreat from its sudden impact, they take refuge in caves; thence the family, thence marriage, thence the second phase. That primeval thunderbolt is first articulated by Joyce on the very first page of *Finnegans Wake*, and it resounds through the first section.[23] What the thunder says in each case varies,[44] but it is invariably a word of one hundred letters,[90] onomatopoetic in effect,[257] enunciating its own name in numerous foreign languages.[332] The magic vocable makes two anti-climatic farewell appearances—as a cough at the beginning of Shaun's fable of the Ondt and the Gracehoper,[414] and as an obscene noise at the end.[424]

Where Vico has distinguished his second phase by the characteristic institution of the family, Joyce dedicates his second section to childhood. The background is a children's party, and the rhythms jingle with games and dances and nursery rhymes. One chapter assumes the format of a textbook, borrowing its imagery from grammar and arithmetic. 'We've had our day at triv and quad and writ our bit as intermidgets.'[306] Now we harken to the tolling of curfew;[244] again, like the infant Stephen in the *Portrait of the Artist*, we stare out at the world from our cradle.[282] 'We are once amore as babes awondering in a wold made fresh where with the hen in the storyaboot we start from scratch.'[336] Still again, as civilization progresses, we attend the sessions of a senate, although we can never be sure whether we are in the Roman Empire or the Irish Free State.[454] The major themes of death and regeneration, the two connotations of *wake*, are insistently voiced in every chapter, but they do not prevail until the funeral services of the third section[499] and the exhumation ceremonies of the fourth.[610] The whole sequence is likely to emerge, coloured by its context, at any moment:[117]

. . . their weatherings and their marryings and their buryings and their natural selections . . .

Or again:[362]

. . . thunderburst, ravishment, dissolution, and providentiality . . .

And again:[614]

. . . eggburst, eggblend, eggburial, and hatch-as-hatch can . . .

We cannot even start to read *Finnegans Wake* without being confronted by an example of the adroit punctilio with which Viconian theory has been translated into Joycean practice. The book opens, as a matter of fact, in the middle of a sentence. For the subject of that sentence we must turn to the end of the book. The final passage—if anything here can be called final—is a continuously flowing, eternally feminine soliloquy, not unlike the concluding episode of *Ulysses*. This time an even more elemental female than Molly Bloom is speaking: it is Anna Livia Plurabelle, the voice of the river Liffey (*amnis Livia*), as she winds along her tortuous course from the nearby Wicklow mountains toward Dublin Bay, and rushes forth at last into the arms of her father, the sea. *Pia et pura bella*—for what it is worth—is Vico's catchphrase for holy wars.[178] The opening sentence completes a transition from the *Ewig-Weibliche* to the masculine principle, and 'brings us by a commodius vicus of recirculation back to Howth Castle and Environs'.

Thus, at the instant of our introduction to his hero and heroine, Joyce has reduced them to their least common denominators; the great castle that dominates the harbour from its promontory at the northern arm, and the little river that wanders across the city of Dublin. The rest is a series of episodes in the long-drawn-out romance between the 'lord of the heights' and the 'lady of the valley'.[501] Henceforth they are to maintain their own cycle of relationships—a tree and a stone, a cloud and a hill, a river and a city. Together they are ultimately reducible to our first parents, Adam and Eve, whom Joyce lists as 'Your Favourite Hero or Heroine'.[306] They comprise the city-building resourcefulness of mankind and the vital fertility of womankind. And, since no extremes of generalization are alien to Joyce, they are likewise civilization and nature, space and time, death and life. The earth itself is suspended from Yggdrasil, the old Germanic tree of knowledge. Symbolism, relegated to the background of *Ulysses*, advances to the foreground of *Finnegans Wake*. As we enter this looking-glass world, we leave reality on the other side. Whereas Bloom and Molly were ordinary mortals re-enacting a myth, Earwicker and his Annie are mythical beings euphemerized.

Before we meet our hero in his human guise, it will be worth our trouble to make a brief tour of his figurative locale. Readers of *Ulysses* will not have forgotten the hill of Howth, for it was here among the rhododendrons that Molly Bloom uttered her throbbing affirmation. Here, in a discarded passage of the *Portrait of the Artist*, the adolescent Stephen once contemplated suicide. Dubliners like to imagine the peninsula as the recumbent figure of a sleeping giant, and the hill as his head. Visitors to the castle are shown relics of Dean Swift—in his day a frequent visitor—and the two-handed twelfth-century sword of its founder, Sir Almeric Tristram.[211] This marauding Norman is said to have acquired the property through the intercession of Saint Lawrence, and in gratitude to have taken the saint's name for his family. Both the saint's name and that of his namesake, the patron saint of Dublin, Lawrence O'Toole, are continually invoked by Joyce.[517] From the first page through the book,[145] the German pronouncement of Saint Patrick himself, *tauf tauf* ('I baptize'),[249] answers the Gaelic supplication of Saint Bridget, *mishe mishe* ('I am').[605]

Sir Almeric's surname, of course, also belongs to a more romantic hero; while the Latin form of his Christian name (Armoricus) suggests the native land of one of that more romantic hero's two heroines, Iseult of Brittany (Armorica).[211] His other heroine, Iseult of Ireland, is connoted by Chapelizod, a small village on the Liffey which forms the setting for Joyce's second section, through another of those verbal coincidences that almost seem to exist for his convenience. It is also the setting for Sheridan Lefanu's faded novel, *The House by the Churchyard*, which gains recognition from Joyce on these grounds.[245] Wagner's leading motives of love and death find their place in Vico's scheme of things, and the first phrase of Isolde's *Liebstod*, '*Mild und leise*', is

'locally known as Mildew Lisa'.[40] Wagner's own Isolde, 'mud-
heeldy wheesindonk' (Mathilde Wesendonck), is the bedraggled
object of a 'trist in Parisise'.[230] Tristan—the Wagnerian spelling
cuts the love story down to its starkest roots, 'Treestone'[113]—is the
hero in his amorous role, though there are occasions when he
seems better qualified for the unromantic part of King Mark.[383]
The two Iseults are his Armorican wife and his daughter Isobel,
'Icy-la-Belle',[246] and their subconscious alternation is one of the
ambiguities of the book. It is scarcely clarified by the presence of
a third heroine, an American niece, who seems to have come
between his wife and his daughter in the catalogue of Earwicker's
loves.[373] It is thoroughly obscured by the theme of the 'prankquean'.[21]

This is based on the anecdote of how a princess of Connaught,
Grace O'Malley (Graine Ni Maille), was denied the hospitality of
Howth Castle one Christmas day, as her ship was sailing home
from a visit to Queen Elizabeth, and how she retaliated by kidnapping a child of the lord of the castle.[115] She is apparently Joyce's
'queen lying abroad from fury of the gales'.[567] His hero in this
episode bears the title of Jarl van Hoother, in which the Norse for
earl is prefixed to a brand of cocoa. He is rather the proprietor of a
public-house than the suzerain of a manor. The riddling question
which the prankquean asks him has many repetitions and variations,[260] but it remains a riddle: [372] 'why . . . do I am alook alike
a poss of porterpease?'[417] At least two clues to its meaning are implicit in its rhythm.[623] Through the prankquean's enigma we hear
the overtones of a customer's request for 'a pot of porter, please'.
Furthermore, her words vibrate to the proverbial expression, 'look
as like as two peas'—which seems to bear another equivocal
reference to the mother-daughter complex.

But we have not yet exhausted the relevant associations of
Howth Castle and environs. The caretaker will show you a cromlech which is believed to have marked the resting place of Dermot
and Grania (Diarmuid and Graine) in their flight from their lord
and master, Finn MacCool (Fionn MacCumhal).[291] Mute stones
conjure up the sad old triangular tale of a Celtic princess, betrothed

to a middle-aged chieftain, eloping with his younger henchman. This earlier Grania, who might just as well have been Iseult or Deirdre or Guinevere, was a daughter of the king of Tara, Cormac Mac Arth, and through epic degeneration a left-handed relative of that prince of cuckolds, King Arthur.[285] Finn was the leader of her father's champions, the Fianna, and Dermot was the most gallant of that band. Finn's least heroic feat, his pursuit of the lovers, is the one that most concerns Joyce. When he displays an interest in Finn's youthful encounter with the Salmon of Wisdom, it is usually in quibbling conjunction with the name of Solomon,[297] and with the Liffey in the neighbourhood of Leixlip (Salmon Leap).[525] A less adulterated account of these legends may be gathered from Lady Gregory's *Gods and Fighting Men*. From Standish O'Grady's apocryphal history of Ireland during the heroic period, we gather occasional glimmerings of *Finnegans Wake*: 'But all around, in surging, tumultuous motion, come and go the gorgeous, unearthly beings that long ago emanated from bardic minds, a most weird and mocking world. Faces rush out of the darkness, and as swiftly retreat again. Heroes expand into giants, and dwindle into goblins, or fling aside the heroic form and gamble as buffoons; gorgeous palaces are blown asunder like a smoke-wreath; buried monarchs reappear. . . .'

Ossian (Oisin) the son of Finn, who outlived his age to tell its tales to Saint Patrick in the elegiac *Colloquy of the Old Men*, was the last of the Fianna. There are those who hold, however, that the Ossianic warriors never died, but still slumber in a cave beneath some hillside, waiting for the awakening that is to redeem Ireland. Joyce's title proclaims Finn's resurgence, as well as the notorious rites of Tim Finnegan, in the Irish-American music-hall ballad, who was brought back to life by a gallon of whisky that missed its aim:

> '*Och, he revives. See how he raises.*'
> *And Timothy, jumping from the bed,*
> *Cried, while he lathered round like blazes,*
> '*Bad luck to your sowls. D'ye think I'm dead?*'

> *Whack, Hurroo. Now dance to your partners,*

> *Welt the flure, your trotters shake;*
> *Isn't it all the truth I've told ye,*
> *Lots of fun at Finnegan's wake?*

'. . . To rise in the world', says the ballad, 'Tim carried a hod.' Evidently the man was a competent artisan, if not a fabulous artificer—a portrait of Dædalus as a bricklayer. He is formally introduced as 'Bygmester Finnegan', in emulation of Ibsen's *Master Builder*.[4] 'Closer inspection of the *bordereau*', Joyce declares, with a sidelong glance at the misleading evidence in the Dreyfus case, 'would reveal a multiplicity of personalities inflicted on the documents.'[107] His protagonist is a host in more ways than one. *Qua* hero he may be Finn, but he is Finnegan as a master builder, Tristan as a lover, Adam as a father, and—of all people— Humpty Dumpty as a sinner. 'Allmen.'[419]

Joyce is by no means unaware of the pitfalls of his syncretic method of characterization: '. . . in this scherzarade of one's thousand one nightinesses that sword of certainty which would indentifide the body never falls.'[51] He has provided a means of identification that is childishly simple. It consists of interweaving through the text the initials of his two symbolic figures: in one instance we read of 'heroticisms, catastrophes, and eccentricities transmitted by the ancient legacy of the past'.[614] Sometimes, as here, these tags are inconspicuously woven into the discourse; sometimes they stand out severely. Without modification, the letters ALP combine to spell the first letter of the primordial Semitic alphabet. 'Haveth Childers Everywhere'[535] is the epithet that designates HCE (or 'Hek') in his patriarchal dignity, and 'Here Comes Everybody'—when it is acrostically compounded of eighteen proper names[88]—suggests his universality. So, when this figure, 'magnificently well worthy of any and all such universalisation',[32] scales down to the dimensions of a contemporary citizen of Dublin, his name is Humphrey Chimpden Earwicker. *Ecce Homo!*

'Wigs on the green', in the hurlyburly of an Irish fight, are transmogrified into 'earwigs on the green'.[47] The earwig is an insect which is popularly supposed to be able to penetrate your brain through the orifice of your ear, and to buzz around inside your head. One of the Roman emperors is reported to have died that way. And, in the sense that Alice's King and Queen of Hearts and all their minions turn out to be nothing but a pack of cards, Joyce's apparitions resolve themselves into a buzzing noise in the mind of the sleeping Humphrey. He survives, but he has a bad night of it. It happens, very neatly for Joyce's purposes, that the habitual motion of earwigs is to fall: you remember them suddenly dropping on your pillow. English children ask each other, 'What does the earwig say when he falls off the table?' The answer, which ought not to abash the reader of Joyce, is ' 'Ere we go!' Because the French call the same insect *perce-oreille*, Joyce has a jocular trick of calling his hero Persse O'Reilly.

Earwicker is really a Scandinavian name, most probably a corruption of the poetic form for Erik (Eirikr); but, by a strained application of Joycean etymology, it can be made to mean 'dweller in Ireland'. It means, at all events, an outsider, a Protestant Irishman of Scandinavian descent. It means that Joyce, the Dubliner in exile, whether he is thinking of Leopold Bloom or Jonathan Swift or even Oliver Cromwell, is always attracted to the outsider in Dublin. His metropolis is always 'Dyoubelong'.[13] Yet Dublin, in contrast to the rest of Ireland, is itself foreign and cosmopolite. Originally a Viking outpost and subsequently an Anglo-Norman garrison, it is aptly represented by a scion of the Vikings and a Norman fortress. And Dublin itself aptly represents the transmutations of history, 'comming nown from the asphalt to the concrete, from the human historic brute, Finnsen Faynean, occeanyclived, to this same vulganized hillsir from yours, Mr. Tupling Toun of Morning de Heights with his lavast flow and his rambling undergroands'.[481] Listen for the radio broadcast from the hill of Howth,[531] for the survey of civilization incorporated in the growth of the city,[540] for the memorable passage which hymns the wedding of the city and the river.[547]

Joyce's books are—as Mann said of *Der Zauberberg*—neither short nor long, but hermetic. We have so little critical equipment for divining a complex piece of symbolism that we may be excused for borrowing the terminology of the Middle Ages. That 'divine comic',[440] Dante Alighieri, explained to Can Grande della Scala that his own work could be interpreted at four different levels, and it may throw some light on *Finnegans Wake* to consider Joyce's 'monomyth'[581] in those terms. Anagogically, it envisages nothing less than the development of civilization, according to Vico's conceptions. Allegorically, it celebrates the topography and atmosphere of the city of Dublin and its environs. Literally, it records the misadventures—or rather the nightmares—of H. C. Earwicker, as he and his wife and three children lie in their beds above his pub, and broken slumber reiterates the events of the day before. Morally, it fuses all these symbols into a central theme, which is incidentally Milton's—the problem of evil, of original sin. 'Of manifest 'tis obedience and the. Flute!'[343] Finnegan, Earwicker, Adam, Lucifer, and Humpty Dumpty are involved in the same fall, and that fall is accompanied by a detonation of Vico's thunder.

The Miltonic struggle is continued on the football field, 'Christ's Church varses Bellial',[301] as Joyce pursues his theme from *Paradise Lost* to *Paradise Regained*, from the local church of Adam and Eve's to Dublin's Eden Quay. His philosophical affiliations forbid him to entertain the notion of a fall, except as the prelude to a rise—whether it be conceived as historical renascence, theological salvation, or merely waking in the morning. The *motif* of the rainbow, appearing to Noah in the aftermath of the flood, is complementary to the thunderbolt; we can dimly descry it, if we read the girls' names on page 227 backwards. Saint Augustine's exclamation of joy over the fall and its consequent promise of grace, *O felix culpa!*, repeats itself in changing forms and contexts. When Joyce exclaims 'O foenix culprit!'[23] over the (moral) downfall of (literal) Earwicker, thereby locating his story in (allegorical) Dublin and adhering to Vico's schedule of (anagogical) revival, he demonstrates how the four levels of symbolism can be subsumed by a single phrase.

The Phoenix Park stretches along the Liffey to the west of Dublin, just beyond the Guinness Brewery and not far below Chapelizod. Anglo-Irish dissensions, incarnate in its Viceregal Lodge and its Wellington Monument, have won Joyce over to

Bonapartism. Its very name is the emblem of his hopes. Ever since *Dubliners* he has thought of Ireland as a land of shades, burying their dead, keening over their lost leader, Parnell. Dublin has become 'Healiopolis'—[24] not so much the Egyptian city of the sun, to which the Arabian phoenix of Herodotus bore the embalmed body of its parent, as the city of Tim Healy, the compromising politician whom Joyce had attacked in his juvenile polemic. Even now, in his literary testament, he cannot forget the fatally mis-spelled word 'hesitancy', which discredited a forged letter in-criminating Parnell in the Phoenix Park murders.[119] Nevertheless, if the rainbow is to shine, if Finn is to wake again, if the Phoenix is to rise from its ashes, the sins of the past must be forgotten. Meanwhile the park, with its convenient serpentine, becomes the Garden of Eden, and the exhibition that Earwicker has made of himself there becomes 'the hubbub caused in Edenborough'.[29]

'In dreams', confessed a connoisseur, Thomas De Quincey, 'perhaps under some secret conflict of the midnight sleeper, lighted up to the consciousness at the time, but darkened to the memory as soon as all is finished, each several child of our mys-terious race completes for himself the treason of the aboriginal fall.' Though the precise nature of Earwicker's original sin, like that of Proust's Albertine, remains uncertain, his behaviour has been calculated to provoke our darkest suspicions, and his night thoughts are haunted by a suggestive sense of guilt. 'We've heard it aye since songdom was gemurrmal.'[251] *Finnegans Wake* is murky with what must be succinctly described as 'cultic twalette'.[344] Tom Sawyer and Huck Finn, before the book has finished with them, have gone far beyond the limits of boyish mischief.[410] In exposing childhood to depravity, Joyce carries 'Mark Time's Finist Joke'[455] too far—far beyond Henry James's 'general vision of evil'. Evils are never nameless; nothing is, with Joyce. They are all very plausibly motivated by the conditions of dream psychology, and they grant him an uproarious opportunity to take his revenge on the censors, but they should not mislead us into taking too sinister a view of the situation.

The latent fantasy of homosexuality and incest, however close to the surface, should be kept on a subliminal Freudian level or sublimated to the plane of primitive myth. Joyce, in the wake of anthropology and psychology, derives social institutions from the family and human relations from sex. True, there may be a lower level of symbolism than those we have been able to explore, on which the characters are bodily organs and the action is straight physiology. Still, the elementary symbols for man and woman are Freud's, a building and a body of water. Exposure to water, Freud has asserted, is the common element in fantasies of birth and myths of the nativity of a hero—Moses and the bulrushes, Finn and the salmon. The folklore themes of kidnapping and elopement travesty the uneasy affections of the sleeper toward his long-suffering wife, his idolized daughter, and his rival sons. Joyce's treatment of motives, moreover, owes more to theology than to psychoanalysis. The inter-relation of his characters, in burlesque scenario, sounds vaguely like the intrigues of New Comedy, but more definitely like those cases of conscience which Jesuits study.[572] He is classical and Catholic in his view of human nature, 'his craft ebbing',[290] in his knowing attempt to read mature corruption back into infant innocence, 'yung and easily freudened',[115] in his evil-minded intrusions upon the sanctity of the family circle: '. . . the nice little smellar squalls in his crydle what the dirtly old bigger'll be squealing through his coughin. . . .'[444]

The unpardonable sin of Hawthorne's *Ethan Brand*, the intellectual pride which inhibits the artist from keeping up 'an intercourse with the world', is strenuously expiated by Joyce's H. C. Earwicker. The responsibility that begins in dreams has all fallen upon his shoulders, for all humanity is one unhappy family, and he is the *paterfamilias*. His case is 'Der Fall Adams'.[70] He is the very genius of paternity whom Stephen Dedalus sought in vain. But it was a young man who wrote the *Portrait of the Artist*; *Ulysses* was being written while Joyce was Bloom's age; and now the author and the hero of *Finnegans Wake* are both 'around fifty'.[506] Stephen's name is Dedalus, after all, and he has now become a family man. Cut off from every other tie, the elderly exile clings closer to his *ménage*. The father feels for his daughter that special relationship which once extended from mother to son: 'sonhusband' seeks 'daughterwife'.[627] To his own sons he hands on the feud between the artist and the city. In his own Dædalean labours he has reached a working agreement: with *Finnegans Wake* the artist has retired into his handiwork. The quest for a father that preoccupied Dostoevsky, through *A Raw Youth*, came to a tragic conclusion in the parricide of *The Brothers Karamazov*. Joyce prefers the artifice of a happy ending: when Icarus discovers Dædalus within himself, he sets out to rebuild his native city, brick by brick.

Face to face with the reality of experience, hammering out the uncreated conscience of his race, Joyce's new paternalistic attitude toward Ireland is Earwicker's attitude toward his sons. The twins are still blue-eyed boys in a crib, sleeping the sleep of the blest, waking fitfully as the 'nightmail' is heard in the morning distance, to be relieved of their childish fears by a word from their parent. 'Sonly all in your imagination, dim. Poor little brittle magic nation, dim of mind.'[565] By a striking series of enlargements the 'Jiminy' (*Gemini*), Jerry and Kevin, are metamorphosed into the Titanic antagonists, Shem and Shaun. Both take after their father, with whom they may be jointly equated. They too embody mankind, but mankind in conflict with itself, Joyce's embodiment of Bruno's dualism. Their opposition, when they 'joustle for that sonneplace'[568] on various levels and under many disguises, lends the book its dynamic force. When they are the outcast Cain and the favourite Abel, they are true children of the first parents. When they are Jacob and Esau, their traits are the traits which Mann delineates in *Die Geschichten Jaakobs*, and their father is the father of the Home Rule movement, Isaac Butt.[3] A name to conjure with, John Jameson, is a potent symbol for this unholy trinity.[126]

From Shem to Seumas to James is an easy modulation for Joyce, and there can be no doubt that the autobiographical interest of the book is centred upon this character, the black sheep of the family. In more than one passage Joyce seems to be announcing—in evasive jargon, to be sure—that he is Shem: 'Immi ammi Semmi.'[258] 'My shemblable! My freer!' he cries, aping Baudelaire's apostrophe to the hypocritical reader.[489] Elsewhere Shem is verbally attached to Dædalus.[179] His characteristic epithet, the souvenir of a once famous Victorian melodrama about a forger in high society, Sir Charles Young's *Jim the Penman*, implies that he is a man of letters.[27] He is the half-mad scribbler, or—in phraseology which Joyce pilfered from Frank Capra's film, *Mr. Deeds Goes to Town*—'the pixillated doodler'.[421] In infantile experimentation, it would seem, he once endeavoured to use his own excrement for ink.[185] His literary habits are catalogued in the unflattering language of harsh experience.[180] The description of his house, 'the Haunted Ink-bottle' is a devastating parody of naturalism.[182] 'Lowness' is the keynote of his character: he is continually being denounced for impiety[187] or for lack of patriotism,[190] or being harangued by his self-satisfied 'doblinganger'.[490] Shem, in short, is an ironically abusive portrait of the artist. 'Do you hold yourself then for some god in the manger, Shehohem, that you will neither serve not [*sic*] let serve, pray nor let pray?'[188]

Shaun (Sean), unlike his 'cerebrated brother',[421] is treated with a proper respect. It is in the cards from infancy that he will enter the Senate (Seanad), or make his fortune in America, or do well by himself in the priesthood. Shaun is seen to the best advantage as Juan,[461] the 'wideheaded boy', the 'embrassador-at-Large',[472] delivering an incredibly blasphemous Lenten sermon to the coy congregation of twenty-nine young ladies. His epithet, 'the Post', implies—among other things—that he is a man of action, 'Jno Citizen'.[447] His quarrel with the man of feeling, 'Jas Pagan', is most sharply stated in a fable from Æsop, which Joyce has converted into a parable of space and time, by crediting the ant and the grasshopper with the respective mentalities of *Verstand* and *Vernunft*. 'For if sciencium (what's what) can mute uns nought, 'a thought, abought the Great Sommbboddy within the Omniboss, perhops an artsaccord (hoot's hoot) might sing ums tumtim abutt the Little Newbuddies that ring his panch.'[415] This is not the philosophy of success. Having 'jingled through a jungle of love and debts and jangled through a jumble of life in doubts',[416] the Gracehoper is put to shame by the worldly wisdom of the Ondt.

Yet it is the artist, 'hoppy on akkant of his joyicity',[414] who has the last word, and rebukes the philistine with an agile series of antithetical couplets:[418]

> *I pick up your reproof, the horsegift of a friend,*
> *For the prize of your save is the price of my spend . . .*
> *Your genus its worldwide, your spacest sublime!*
> *But, Holy Saltmartin, why can't you beat time?*

If all men are brothers, then their natural state is fratricidal warfare. The decisive battles of *Finnegans Wake*—perhaps for no better reason than a bad chromo or a worse pun—are those of the Crimean War.[334] The mere name of Inkerman is a talisman for Joyce.[48] The story of how a certain Buckley shot a Russian general is mysteriously implicated in the gossip about Earwicker's crime.[101] The historic escapades of a minor hero, Lieutenant Buckley of H.M.S. *Miranda*, who won the Victoria Cross for firing Cossack stores during the siege of Sebastopol, scarcely seem to warrant so many whispers and snickers. The last governor-general of Ireland, Donal Buckley ('Don Gouverneur Buckley'[375]), scarcely commands more attention. History offers a more intriguing figure in Captain Nolan of the Fifteenth Hussars, who was immortalized in Tennyson's line, 'Some one had blunder'd.'[474] He paid for the blunder by death, soon after his gesture of insubordination had misdirected the charge of the light brigade, but we read in Kinglake's *Invasion of the Crimea* that the corpse went on riding and shouting. We read of a letter to Nolan's mother, borne by a wounded messmate through the battle of Balaklava. Is this Joyce's 'untitled mamafesta'?[104] *Nolens volens*, 'brigadier-general Nolan' expresses the *non serviam* of the rebel poet, while 'buccaneer-admiral Browne' reasserts the everlasting yea of his compliant twin.[567]

It is the old problem of the many and the one. The Russian general, *alias* 'General Jinglesome',[229] *alias* 'Mr Jinglejoys',[466] may well be Shem, whose writing is caviar to the general. Buckley, pronounced somewhat like the Gaelic *bouchalleen bawn* ('fair-haired *boy*') may again be Shaun, taking his stand for young Ireland.[220] Penman and Post, whether on the battlefield or in the nursery, are the writer and the bearer of a message. Their epithets, beyond an obviously phallic significance, are even more intimately related. They relate the devilish twins to the affair of the letter—the lost letter from another world in which so many of the secrets of the book seem to have been sealed. This may have been quite an ordinary communication, with news of a wedding and a funeral and other family matters, addressed to Annie by a semi-literate lady named Maggie from Boston, Mass., which turned up on a dunghill and fell into the claws of a neighbour's chicken.[111] It may not inconceivably have been what is known in England as a 'French letter' and in France as a *capote anglaise*.[575] On the other hand, it may be the profession of letters, the art and mystery of literature, from alpha to omega.[94] It may prove to be the handwriting on the wall, [18] and its three concluding X's may be hieroglyphics, awaiting the scrutiny of some future Champollion.[11] Annie is frankly puzzled by it: 'Every letter is a hard but yours sure is the hardest crux ever.'[623]

Difficult to elucidate, certainly, yet not different in kind from the experiments of other writers. Not more hybrid than the five books of Rabelais, nor—to come nearer home with an Anglo-Irish analogy—more discursive than Sterne. 'Nothing odd will live long,' Dr. Johnson warned seekers after literary novelty in 1776. '*Tristram Shandy* did not last.' Joyce's work, to our surprise and encouragement, has many such analogies. The phoenix is always a rare bird, but never an extinct species. The class of unclassifiable books is a well-recognized *genre*, particularly in English: *Finnegans Wake* belongs on a shelf with *The Anatomy of Melancholy, Don Juan, Sartor Resartus, Moby-Dick,* and *The Golden Bough*. Looking for prototypes, after Joyce's fashion, we come remarkably close with Nashe's inimitable version of the tragedy of Hero and Leander, told in terms of the rivalry between the herring fisheries of Yarmouth and Lowestoft. The *ad hoc* invention of a polyglot style was contrived as long ago as the fifteenth century by the macaronic school. And it was presumably a countryman of Joyce's, some whimsical monkish rhetorician of the eleventh century, who perpetrated the *Hisperica Famina*—that curious miscellany of acrostic hymns, Pythagorean tables, and precious descriptions of commonplace objects, written in the most cryptic vocabulary that the Latin glossaries of his day could furnish.

But, from first to last, it is the other great prose master of Dublin who has left his mark on nearly every page of Joyce's book. Swift —who was born in the same year as Vico and died of the same disease, senile dementia[172]—likewise presides over the mythology of *Finnegans Wake*. He oscillates back and forth between the 'sosie sesthers',[3] Stella and Vanessa. His unmistakable voice breaks in when we least expect it, nagging Esther Johnson in as high a key as Yeats's *Words upon the Window-pane*.[144] His pet name for her, 'Ppt', is the father's name for his daughter,[14] and the girl's for her doll.[588] The cry of the Australian whippoorwill, 'more pork',[359] is transposed to 'Moor Park',[433] the estate of Sir William Temple where Swift suffered his early humiliations.[449] Joyce's mouthpiece, Shem, is clearly to be identified with Swift: the two are consubstantial in 'Mr. O'Shem the Draper'.[421] And the Dean of Saint Patrick's is a model as well as a theme. We have only to recall the puns, jingles, and *pastiches* that interlard his miscellanies, the conscientiously recorded *clichés* of *Polite Conversation*, the 'little language' of the *Journal to Stella*, or the letter to Dr. Sheridan that looks like English and reads like Latin.

*The Tale of a Tub* might be narrated of Shem and Shaun. The dialogue between the spider and the bee, in *The Battle of the Books*, might be pitched in the idiom of the Dublin streets. The *Modest Proposal* is modest indeed, when compared with some of Joyce's suggestions. The little people of Lilliput, the coarse creatures of Brobdingnag, and the learned zanies of Lagado live again in *Finnegans Wake*. Besides bad dreams and mystifications and masquerades, besides their mutual fascination with language, Joyce and Swift have in common a controlled style and an uncontrollable imagination, a disposition to take trifles seriously and to trifle with serious things. Personally, they seem to possess the same sensitive ear for dissonances, the same delicate nose for ordures, the same acute perception of incongruities; the same dehumanized rigour in pursuing a point; the same unabashed familiarity in confiding details; the same strange blend of misanthropic sentimentality and humanitarian detachment. It can be, and often is, said of most artists that they project upon the surfaces of the outer world their inner conflicts and private frustrations. But of what other English writers could it be said that the conflicts were so tense, the frustrations so embittered, or the projections so dazzling and far-flung?

# 2. *The Language of the Outlaw*

Thinking of Swift, said Thackeray, is like thinking of an empire falling. To think about Joyce is to allow our thoughts to dwell upon a buried city. As they have traversed the stages of his career, we have seen the soaring aspirations of young Icarus lead to the underground labyrinth of the ageing Dædalus. We see how his subject broadens as his style darkens: the hero of the *Portrait of the Artist* is the author, the hero of *Ulysses* the common man, of *Finnegans Wake* mankind. The past which Joyce tries to recapture, in the throes of his 'traumaturgid'[496] nightmare, is not personal reminiscence but collective experience. The burial mound of his sleeping giant contains an enormous and heterogeneous time capsule. H. C. Earwicker's subconscious mind is the historical consciousness of the human race. Thus modern culture, rounding out Vico's cycle, cowers before the thunder and returns to the cave—to Plato's cave *via* Saint Patrick's purgatory.[80] With contemporary ruins accumulating above ground, we seek refuge in the underworld of Homeric shades, in the eternal places of Dante's hell, in Shakespeare's dark backward and abysm of time, in the subterranean passages of Sir Thomas Browne, in the hollow caverns under Wagner's foreboding earth, in Lewis Carroll's rabbit-hole of fantasy, Henry James's deep well of memory, T. S. Eliot's contrived corridors of history, or Thomas Mann's *coulisses* and abysses of the past.

Happily, an Irish wake is apt to rise above its melancholy occasion. Here is Joyce talking to himself:[189]

Sniffer of carrion, premature gravedigger, seeker of the nest of evil in the bosom of a good word, you, who sleep at our vigil and fast for our feast, you with your dislocated reason, have cutely foretold, a jophet in your own absence, by blind poring upon your many scalds and burns and blisters, impetiginous sore and pustules, by the auspices of that raven cloud, your shade, and by the auguries of rooks in parlament, death with every disaster, the dynamatisation of colleagues, the reducing of records to ashes, the levelling of all customs by blazes, the return of a lot of sweettempered gun-powdered didst unto dudst but it never stphruck your mudhead's obtundity (O hell, here comes our funeral! O pest, I'll miss the post!) that the more carrots you chop, the more turnips you slit, the more murphies you peel, the more onions you cry over, the more bullbeef you butch, the more mutton you crackerhack, the more potherbs you pound, the fiercer the fire and the longer your spoon and the harder you gruel with more grease to your elbow the merrier fumes your new Irish stew.

The parenthesis is the outcry of the great writer who has come too late. In the times of the Tuatha De Danaan, the legendary tribe that left Greece to colonize Ireland and to be driven into the hills by the later conquests of the Celts, he might have been the Dagda, their poet, priest, and king, whose harp enchanted all his listeners and whose appetite was equal to untold messes of pottage. In a time when universities are bombed and books are burned, the confiscation of the banned English edition of *Ulysses* by the New York post office authorities is an omen of 'the levelling of all customs by blazes'. The last of the bards, half blinded and long exiled, Shem stirs a magic cauldron at the funeral feast of civilization. His international *potpourri* is brewed from an Irish recipe, with a dash of everything else he has ever read or heard. *Ulysses* is seasoned with the same ingredients, but *Finnegans Wake* is the richer concoction. The old themes of the artist and the city are combined in the person of the mythical hod-carrier, the builder of cities. Dublin is now merely the local habitation for history itself. Artifice, by a supreme effort, is bent upon creating a language of its own.

The thwarted filial impulse, still prompting Joyce to look up to some intellectual godfather, goes beyond Homer to the scholar who refined Homer out of existence, beyond the authority of Aquinas to the scepticism of Bruno, and beyond Shakespeare's immediacy to Swift's detachment. If a poet is a maker, a prose writer is *altus prosator*—in the Latin of a venerable Irish hymn attributed to Saint Columba—the sublime begetter.[185] As the son becomes a father, he ceases to be a disciple and becomes a rival. Like 'Great Shapesphere',[295] he emulates God and rivals nature. The note of banishment, which Stephen Dedalus overheard in Shakespeare, is sounded defiantly. The reception of *Ulysses* has lengthened the distance between Joyce and Ireland, or any other English-speaking country. Ruefully, in *Finnegans Wake*, he glances back at 'his usylessly unreadable Blue Book of Eccles'.[179] There are moments of startling candour, when he doubts his mission and questions himself: 'Was liffe worth leaving?'[230] Or conversely, *à la Henri Quatre*, 'was Parish worth thette mess.'[199] When he addressed his friend, John Sullivan, whose remarkably pure tenor range was better appreciated abroad than at home, it was 'a Banned Writer to a Banned Singer'. So much public apathy and so little critical discernment, together with such excruciating treatment at the hand of the publishers and censors, tangibly reinforced his sense of persecution. 'A hundred cares, a tithe of troubles,' moans the river, 'and is there one who understands me?'[627]

Since Joyce lived to write, though he never wrote for a living, he went on writing to please himself, with an almost paranoid disregard of any other reader. The authors of the so-called *Exagmination*, it must be acknowledged, were more of a *claque* than an audience, like Victor Hugo's friends on the first night of *Hernani*. Yet Joyce's disregard was touchingly sensitive to the slightest sign of outside interest. His friends report that his last year was clouded by the indifferent response to *Finnegans Wake*—as if it could have been otherwise. The indifference was quite natural, and so was his disappointment. What was unnatural is that he should have cultivated both for seventeen years 'with a meticulosity bordering on the insane'.[173] His work in progress he came to regard as 'that letter selfpenned to one's other, that neverperfect everplanned'.[489] To be a writer under such circumstances, for Shakespeare, would have meant 'speechless death'; for Joyce's garrulous fellow Parisian, Gertrude Stein, it meant a chance to be 'alone with English'.

For Joyce, exile meant a renewal of silence and, under the tutelage of the Defence of the Realm Act, a new and diabolical cunning: 'Mum's for's maxim, ban's for's book and Dodgesome Dora for hedgehung sheolmastress.'[228]

The silence behind *Finnegans Wake*, like the silence that Carlyle preached in forty volumes, is the oracular sort that requires comment. Having abandoned his hopes of direct communication, Joyce turned his efforts to symbolic expression. 'In a Symbol there is concealment and yet revelation,' opined Carlyle's oracle, Dr. Teufelsdroeckh, 'hence, therefore, by Silence and by Speech acting together, comes a double significance.' But this augmented meaning will be hardly audible to those whose patience is not intrigued by the metaphorical diction of Vico's heroic age. To say that Joyce's writing smells of the lamp is to make a pallid understatement. It reeks of the thurible. No writer, not Flaubert himself, has set a more conspicuous example of the cult of style. Joyce's holy grail, *la dive bouteille*, is Shem's inkbottle. For its sake he has given up his church along with his city, and by its virtue he would recover them. In the discipline and tradition of literature, perhaps, he finds compensations for the rootlessness of his life. 'Suffoclose! Shikespower! Seudodanto! Anonymoses!' he exclaims, transported by his own ingenuity.[47] He has identified himself with the greatest writers; he has recapitulated the development of English prose; now he must synthesize his language.

English was only an acquired speech to the artist as a young man. Latin was an educational and ecclesiastical idiom. Gaelic was one of those nets that Stephen flew by. The hard years of Trieste and Zürich were weathered by teaching English and other foreign languages in the cosmopolitan babel of the Berlitz schools. Joyce's synthetic language had to distort, if not disown, the tongue of Shakespeare and Swift; it had to preserve the hieratic intonations of the liturgy, excite the enthusiasms of a literary movement, and reverberate with the polyglot humours of the professional linguist. To fulfil these conditions, it had to assume what I. A. Richards calls a severance of poetry and belief: it had to be 'sanscreed'.[215] A ripe specimen of patriotic eloquence, quoted in the newspaper episode of *Ulysses*,[132] compares the plight of the Jews under the Pharaohs to that of Ireland in the British Empire. *'Why will you jews not accept our culture, our religion and our language?'* the high priest asks Moses. The answer, when Joyce himself declaims it, even through the imperfections of an acoustical recording, is his *apologia* for the nomadic life of the banished writer. His expatriation is an exodus, a deliverance from slavery. The bearer of the curse is destined to be the bringer of the word:

—*But, ladies and gentlemen, had the youthful Moses listened to and accepted that view of life, had he bowed his head and bowed his will and bowed his spirit before that arrogant admonition, he would never have brought the chosen people out of their house of bondage nor followed the pillar of the cloud by day. He would never have spoken with the Eternal amid lightnings on Sinai's mountaintop nor ever have come down with the light of inspiration shining in his countenance and bearing in his arms the tables of the law, graven in the language of the outlaw.*

Saint Patrick, who spent forty days on a mountain in his turn, fasting and praying for the conversion of Ireland, stands by the side of Moses in the hierarchy of *Finnegans Wake*.[307] Here the implied relation of the Irish to the Israelites is that of Stephen to Bloom, of artist to prophet. Inspiration, in the most transcendental sense of the word, holds both terms of the comparison together. A work of art, according to those tenets of esthetic mysticism which Joyce so devoutly professed, is among the varieties of religious experience. His earliest sketches were epiphanies and his choice of a career was a kind of ordination. His maturest work still conforms to the Catholic pattern: as Valery Larbaud observed, it is closer to the Jesuit casuists than to the French naturalists. And, if Joyce's naturalism seems to stem from the confessional, we may also observe that his symbolism is deeply rooted in the sacrament of the mass. The black mass of *Ulysses* follows the *confiteor* of the *Portrait of the Artist*. The hero of *Finnegans Wake*, in the character of a cricketer named 'Hosty', is again united with the body of Christ. 'How culious an epiphany!'[508] The church is broad enough to touch the extremes of confession and mystery, both the appalling frankness and the laboured obscurity with which Joyce alternately expresses himself. As the artist's stature enlarges, he is no longer a visionary but a demiurge, no longer waiting for revelations but arranging them. With godlike equivocation he can reveal or conceal, mystify or make manifest, fashion myths and forge words.

Words are the stuff that Earwicker's dream is made on. The darker shadings of consciousness, the gropings of the somnolent mind, the states between sleeping and waking—unless it be by Proust—have never been so acutely rendered. But Joyce's technique always tends to get ahead of his psychology. *Finnegans Wake* respects, though it garbles and parodies, the literary conventions. It brims over with *ad libs* and misplaced confidences and self-conscious stage-whispers. Now and then it pauses to defend itself,[112] to bait the censorship,[179] or to pull the legs of would-be commentators.[453] It mentions the working title,[497] throws in such items as 'The Holy Office'[190] and 'Gas from a Burner',[93] and freely discusses the suppression of *Dubliners*.[185] It includes a brief outline of *Ulysses*[229] and even a letter to the author from a dissatisfied reader.[113] In reply, frequent telegraphic appeals from the author to his 'abcedminded' readers[18] ('. . . stop, please stop, do please stop, and O do please stop respectively . . .'[124]) punctuate[232] the torrent[379] of his soliloquy[560] periodically.[609] These *obiter dicta* cannot be traced, with any show of plausibility, to the sodden brain of a snoring publican. No psychoanalyst could account for the encyclo-pedic sweep of Earwicker's fantasies or the acoustical properties of his dream-work.

The strangest feature of this dream vision is that it lacks visual imagery. Joyce's imagination, as his light is spent, concentrates on the 'mind's ear'.[477] Though he offers us a *'verbivocovisual presentment'*,[341] it is no easier to visualize a Mookse or a Gripes than to gather a clear-cut impression of slithy tove or a mome rath. 'Ope Eustace tube!' is his sound advice.[535] When he promises us a view of Dublin, he enjoins us to listen: 'Hush! Caution! Echoland!'[13] The isle is full of noises. Gradually, after we have become accustomed to the darkness, we recognize familiar voices. From the pedantic jargon[121] and childish lisping,[396] the young men's blarney[407] and old women's chatter,[101] we distinguish Earwicker by his intermittent stutter[45] and catastrophic hiccup.[454] He is usually submerged in a welter of dialects and documents—pidgin English,[485] American slang,[455] vulgar Latin,[185] liturgical responses,[470] legal forms,[545] advertisements,[181] riddles.[170] To this confusion of tongues the radio lends a spasmodic continuity, comparable to the influence of the film on *Ulysses*. The loudspeaker, with its summons to sales and revolutions, its medley of raucous chamber music and prefabricated repartee, its collaboration between Dædalean engineering and blind static, is the medium of *Finnegans Wake*. With a 'tolvtubular high fidelity dialdialler',[309] we tune in on the 'sponsor programme' from Howth Castle, 'Haveth Childers Everywhere'.[531]

Everyone who has played Joyce's captivating phonograph record from 'Anna Livia Plurabelle' will agree that the best introduction to his book is to hear him read it aloud. Yet even the author's expressive brogue cannot convey all the inflections, unless it is supplemented by the text. If he ever appeals to the eye, it is to the eye of a reader. A full reading must be simultaneously oral and literary, 'synopticked on the word',[367] dividing our attention between vocal and verbal images. Joyce is interested in both the sound of a word and the figure it cuts on the page. In a disquisition on the alphabet, when he tells us 'how hard a thing it is to mpe mporn a gentlerman', he would remind us that, since *beta* has the value of V in modern Greek, B must be indicated by a *mu* and a *pi*.[120] When he speaks of school days, his book takes on the temporary appearance of a schoolbook. One set of marginalia, in pompous capitals, exhibits Vico's terminology. The other set, in shrewd italics, betrays Joyce's own accents. The footnotes are infantile *scholia*. 'Traduced into jingish janglage for the nusances of dolphins born' recalls the *in usum Delphini* of an edition of the classics notorious for its expurgations.[275] A geometrical diagram demonstrates the equivalence of one delta-shaped triangle lettered ALP to another, or of mother to daughter.[293] An uncivil nose and a pair of crossbones, childishly scrawled at the end of the chapter, are the least abstruse of Joyce's symbols.

The impatient reader, perpetually admonished to look out for typographical ambushes and to keep listening for surreptitious rhythms, may come to feel that *Finnegans Wake* is a grim business. Actually it is a wonderful game—by no means a private affair, but one in which many may join, each with his own contribution, and the more the merrier. This realization may prove equally disturbing to the reader whose conception of art is rather grim. He should realize that all art is a game, the object of which is to make the problems of life and death—with as much insight, skill, and originality as possible—a source of enjoyment. For enjoying *Finnegans Wake*, we need scarcely insist, the prerequisite is not omniscience. It is no more than a curiosity about Joyce's unique methods and some awareness of his particular preoccupations. His work is enriched by such large resources of invention and allusion that its total effect is infinite variety. But, when we are able to scan the variety, we notice that it is controlled by a few well-defined themes and a number of characteristic devices. Myriads of minute details boil down to a handful of generalizations.

The very reverse, of course, is true of the process of composition: it takes the bare elements and exposes them to unceasing elaboration. Writing is primarily a basis for rewriting, and revision is a form of self-caricature. Every word of the first draft is subject to a series of gross exaggerations. Each successive version, even after publication, is a palimpsest for further accretions. We can well believe that the final version of one chapter, previously published as 'Anna Livia Plurabelle', cost Joyce more than 1,600 intensive working hours. His 'warping process'[497] enables him to expand and condense at a single stroke; the alteration of a letter will widen the orbit of a phrase. By including all the alternatives, rather than choosing and discarding, he eliminates the writer's chief torture, hesitation between phrases. Incidentally, he throws economy to the winds. Since the essence of his method is not to select but to accumulate, his readers seldom have that feeling of inevitability which is the touchstone of a more reserved style. They feel a continual surprise. Sooner or later, they feel the reservation voiced by Dr. Johnson, when he said of James Macpherson's earlier attempt to revive the spirit of Finn MacCool: 'Sir, a man might write such stuff for ever, if he would *abandon* his mind to it.'

The differences in mood between *Ulysses* and *Finnegans Wake* are underlined by the contrast between the Homeric poems and that prodigious literary hoax, 'Makefearsome's Ocean'.[294] Joyce's recourse to the Ossianic poems, like his use of the counterfeit word, 'hesitancy', evinces a growing addiction to the idea of forgery. Jim the Penman is forging, with a vengeance, the uncreated conscience of his race. His creative ideals have found their unforeseen fulfilment in 'an epical forged cheque on the public for his own private profit'.[181] The artist, god of his own world, is no better than a criminal in this one, Joyce obliquely admits; the finest literary imitations of life are fakes. It should be unnecessary to add that the only person who has the right to accuse Joyce of being 'a low sham'[170] is himself, and that his accusation is a self-searching testimonial of sincerity. However unintelligible he may seem, he is never incoherent. His idiom is based on a firm command of the usages of popular speech. His habit of sudden generalization is backed by his facility with proverbs. Look at Shem's 'bodily getup': 'all ears, . . . not a foot to stand on, a handful of thumbs, . . . a deaf heart, a loose liver, . . . a manroot of all evil. . . .'[169]

Consciously, by extending his range of reference, Joyce limits our appreciation of his work. Because *po-russki* means 'in Russian' in Russian, 'Paud the russky' is at once an apology for, and an explanation of, a macaronic Anglo-Russian interlude about the Crimean War.[335] 'Pratschkats at their platschpails', for old women by the Liffey, is wasted on us, if we do not know that '*prachka*' and '*plach*' are Russian for 'laundress' and 'crying'.[101] But the words we know should teach us not to conclude, from the words we miss, that Joyce can be vague or loose. Whenever we happen to catch the overtones, we are impressed by his philological accuracy and logical rigour. With *Finnegans Wake* the circular exposition of *Ulysses* is carried to its logical conclusion, which is no conclusion at all. The peculiarity of Joyce's later writing is that any passage presupposes a reading knowledge of the rest of the book. On the other hand, to master a page is to understand the book. The trick is to pick out a passage where a break-through can be conveniently effected. For this sort of exercise, such set-pieces as the 'Tales Told of Shem and Shaun' are both revealing and entertaining. 'When a part so ptee does duty for the holos we soon grow to use of an allforabit.'[18]

A book must have a beginning, a middle and an end; but a dream may be a jumble of excluded middles. The first page of *Finnegans Wake* is an orderly thematic statement, and the following pages bring their own tautologies and *encores*. But the reader must be prepared for continuous digression, instead of consecutive narration. Instead of a table of contents, he may take his bearings from a rough summary of the miscellaneous chapters. The first episode of the first section is an epical invocation;[3] the second episode sets Earwicker's peccadillo to the ribald strains of 'The Ballad of Persse O'Reilly';[30] the third prolongs the hearsay after closing hours;[48] and the fourth proceeds with due solemnity, to the trial.[75] All four are unified by the theme of Earwicker's fall; the fifth episode takes up the question of Anna's letter.[104] The sixth consists of twelve leading questions and evasive answers, passing in review the hero (HCE), the heroine (ALP), their tavern (the Bristol), their city (Dublin), their man of all work (Joe), their maid of all work (Kate), their twelve patrons (variously denominated Murphys, Doyles, or Sullivans), their daughter (Isabel), the theory of history (Vico), the theory of love (Swift), the theory of time and space (illustrated by Shem's fable of the Mookse and the Gripes), and the signature of the author ('*Semus sumus!*') respectively. Shem is the villain of the next episode, unmasked by his twin in an allegorical debate between Justius and Mercius.[169] The rhythm of the river, emerging toward the end of the seventh, is fully orchestrated in the eighth episode, the haunting 'Anna Livia Plurabelle' colloquy.[196]

There are four lengthening episodes to the second section, and again to the third. If a dream may be assigned to a definite location, the first section was located in and around the Phoenix Park; the second is at Chapelizod, and the third will be on the hill of

Howth. The second section starts to be the programme of a play, 'The Mime of Mick, Nick, and the Maggies', with cast, credits, and a lively synopsis.[219] When the diversion ends in a thunderstorm, the party retreats into the book of childhood.[260] The third episode takes us on a voyage of discovery, with the patrons of Earwicker's pub as Viking seafarers.[309] The fourth eavesdrops upon the romance of Tristan and Isolde, through the censorious ears of the quartet of old men ('Mamalujo').[383] After the watchman has told the hour, the third section gives Shaun a chance to tell his fable of the Ondt and the Gracehoper.[403] He is back again, in a second episode, with his sermon.[429] Shaun, by now 'Yawn', is his father's boy, and his 'dream monologue' leads naturally to Earwicker, as Shem's has led to his mother. The third episode marks the climax with a keen over the barrow of the hero.[474] The fourth, a half-waking evocation of the slumbering household, should be carefully scrutinized for its clues to the literal situation.[555] The fourth section is a brief *coda*, which heralds the dawn and completes the Viconian revolution.[593]

This enumeration, if it clarifies anything, confronts us with something more like vaudeville than narrative. The deafmute dialogue of a prehistoric comedy team, Mutt and Jute,[16] is revived on the day of judgement by Muta and Juva,[609] and provides a *divertissement* by Butt and Taff in the midst of the battle of Sebastopol.[338] The tabloid scandal of 'Peaches' and 'Daddy' Browning is warmed over to suit Earwicker's fancy.[65] One red herring after another, pursued by the dreamer, turns out to be an *idée-fixe*. While the main themes are never absent from the background, the foreground is always crowded with topical matters. In the middle distance, ordinarily the centre of interest, the action is shadowy and capricious. Avid for a story, the reader will find little in Joyce's 'meandertale'[18] to reward his pains. He will track down Saint Michael and Satan to their picture-frame on the wall of Earwicker's bedroom, and rationalize the Garden of Eden into a mantelpiece in the Adelphian style of the brothers Adam.[559] The penultimate episode, he will find, is as detailed a survey of domestic arrangements as the corresponding inventory of *Ulysses*. He will find a more substantial residue of human sympathy in the most tenuous sketch of *Dubliners* than in the whole of *Finnegans Wake*.

And tastes will differ, when he complains of being given an intolerable deal of sack to wash down his halfpennyworth of bread. The richness of Joyce's symbolism helps us to tolerate the realities of the situation. Considered for its vestiges of naturalistic fiction, a night with the Earwickers is weary, flat, and stale. Its most dramatic event, signalized by the vulgar name of a quaint fountain in Brussels,[267] occurs when a child wets his bed.[427] Its *dénouement* is the interruption of Earwicker's connubial performance by a rooster,[595] whose chiliastic 'cocorico' is anticipated by numerous alliterations in K.[193] Joyce's perverse passion for the inert and the undistinguished could not have directed him to a less eventful subject. Nor could he, having sacked history and despoiled language, have endowed this unpromising material with more liveliness and distinction. From his own Olympian imaginative level, he causes the all but unmentionable trivialities of daily and nightly routine to produce earth-shaking consequences. Earwicker's flatulence produces Vico's thunder.[258] Pedestrian readers will not forgive a novelist or a dramatist for such conceits, though they accept them from a humorist or even a poet. When we come to sum up Joyce's work, however, we must admit that it was never strong in scenic description, sympathetic characterization, or the other virtues of the novel. His peculiar strength lay in speculation, introspection, and an almost hyperesthetic capacity for rendering sensations. These are poetic attributes, and his successes are the achievements of a poet—in arranging verbal harmonies and touching off emotional responses.

Joyce demands the same degree of absorption that Yeats and Donne receive. We are bound to be disappointed, if we approach him with the notion of extracting a quintessential content from the encumbrances of form. The two, in *Ulysses*, were intended to coalesce. Where they fail to do so, it is because he has imposed a formal requirement that is too rigid to be satisfied without hindering the advance of the plot. The Siren episode is too cluttered up with verbiage to be an effective scene, and too broken up with comment to be an authentic fugue. The drastic solution of this dilemma, in *Finnegans Wake*, is to subordinate content to form: to forgo the normal suspenses and sympathies that bind the reader to the book, reduce the plot to a few platitudes that can be readily stylized, and confer complete autonomy upon words. They are now matter, not manner. Nothing could be farther from the fallacy of imitative form than Joyce's latter tendency toward abstract content. We are borne from one page to the next, not by the expository current of the prose, but by the harmonic relations of the language —phonetic, syntactic, or referential, as the case may be. The mythological themes, recurring, varying, modulating into a new context, have a consistency of their own. When we have an index to them, we shall comprehend the book.

The relation between chapters is abrupt and arbitrary, as with the movements of a symphony. As with music, as with any composition in time, the structure seems to dissolve into the texture, when we examine it closely. At close range, *Finnegans Wake* seems to realize the aspiration of the other arts toward the condition of music. The obvious musical analogies are misleading, for they imply a limitation, rather than an enlargement, of our means of expression. They encourage a doctrine of pure poetry, or prose that exists solely for the sake of euphony. Joyce is a consummate master of the music of words, but he is also a master of 'the music of ideas', the complex orchestration of associated images which symbolist poets have taught us to appreciate. His innovation is to harmonize the two modes. Now, when you bring discordant sounds and associations together, you have created a pun. If the associations remain irrelevant, it is a bad pun; if they show an unlooked-for relevance, it is better; if the relevant associations are rich enough, it is poetry. The Elizabethans regarded this as a legitimate rhetorical resource. The Victorians degraded it into a parlour trick. Joyce has rehabilitated the pun for literary purposes. Again, as he was fond of pointing out, he has a theological precedent: the church itself was founded on a pun ('thuartpeatrick'[3]).

Having laid down such vast reserves of potential association, Joyce can easily and adroitly pun his way through 628 pages.

From Saint Peter and his rock, on one excursion, he can move on to a Greek wine, by a devious route that stops at Petrarch, Laura, laurel, Daphne, and Mavrodaphne.[203] Often these roundabout progressions, like the motions of the mind, disclose unexpected short-cuts. Who would have expected the initial letter of 'victory', translated into Morse code and timed to the opening bar of Beethoven's *Fifth Symphony*, to become a symbol by which millions live and die? The dream convention is Joyce's licence for a free association of ideas and a systematic distortion of language. Psychoanalysis insinuates its special significances into his calculated slips of the tongue. Under cover of a drowsy indistinctness and a series of subconscious lapses, he has developed a diction that is actually alert and pointed, that bristles with virtuosity and will stoop to any kind of slapstick. His neologism is the joint product of the three types of verbal wit that Freud has discriminated—condensation, displacement, allusion.

Joyce perceived that all attempts to make the subconscious intelligible break down into nonsense. This, of course, did not deter him. He perfected a species of 'double-talk', like the convincing gibberish of certain comedians, superficially adjusted to the various norms of discourse, and fundamentally nonsensical. The twofold ambiguity is that, by playfully harping on his obsessions, Joyce makes a modicum of sense. He can contradict himself with a clear conscience and a straight face. Consider his most sustained *double-entendre*: Shaun preaching a sermon on chastity to twenty-nine adolescent girls is really Earwicker professing a more than fatherly love for his daughter. The psychological censor has dictated a sanctimonious tone, and the chapter is scrupulously modelled on the soundest lenten homilectics; but prurience will out. 'Oop, I never open momouth but I pack mefood in it,' Shaun leers genially.[437] Recommending safe books for the *jeune fille*—to quote one of his few safe examples—he debauches the household words of Dickens into 'Doveyed Covetfilles' and 'the old cupiosity shape'.[434] After the sermon in the *Portrait of the Artist*, and the youthful tragedy of Stephen's first recoil from carnal sin, Jaunty Jaun's homily comes as a monstrous satyr-play.

How did Joyce manage to concoct these 'messes of mottage?'[183] By accentuating the purely formal values of words, and by linking them together with as many devices as he could manipulate. Some of these devices are auditory—rhyme,[371] alliteration,[250] assonance,[216] onomatopoeia.[258] Others are morphological—back-formations,[266] infixes,[191] etymologies,[120] spoonerisms.[189] Others are alphabetical—acrostics,[88] anagrams,[140] palindromes,[496] inversions.[311] Still others, more sportive, run through a sequence of words by changing a letter at a time,[142] or weave groups of related names into narratives—one still runs across specimens of this *genre* in school magazines. The material ranges the Joycean gamut from Irish counties ('cold airs')[595] to Ibsen's plays ('peers and gints')[540] and musicians ('pere Golazy' and 'mere Bare').[360] Insects and philosophers collaborate in the cosmic irony of the Ondt and the Gracehoper, by this procedure, and hundreds of rivers accommodate themselves to the main stream of the Liffey. Other devices are peculiar to Joyce—like the four polysyllables terminating in the pretentious suffix-*ation*, which he employs now and then to call the discussion to order.[372]

The official guide to his vocabulary is Lewis Carroll's student of semantics, Humpty Dumpty, who could explain all the poems that were ever invented and a good many that hadn't been just yet. Through 'portmanteau-words' Joyce is able to instil a Freudian undertone in his small-talk. The extra compartment permits the transient word to assimilate local colour: a Siberian atmosphere turns the Bristol into an 'isbar' and the *spécialité de la maison* into 'irsk irskusky'.[70] 'Potapheu's wife' lends a touch of domestic warmth to an otherwise chilling story.[193] The adjective, 'lidylac', applied to curtains, has an appropriate aroma of lavender and old lace.[461] And what better word than 'umbroglia' could have been coined to fit the foreign policy of the late Neville Chamberlain?[284] 'Umprumptu'[93] colours Humpty Dumpty's fall with a tinge of onomatopoetic spontaneity; 'wenchyoumaycuddler' is more specific than it sets out to be.[608] A typical phrase, which telescopes Joyce's prepossessions, is 'viceking's graab': Ireland is both the grave of Norse heroes and the spoil of the British viceroy.[18] When, 'by the waters of babalong', we sit down and laugh, we are exiled to that border region which is disputed by wit and poetry.[103] 'The flush-pots of Euston and the hanging garments of Marylebone' have a retrospective poignance that is not unworthy of T. S. Eliot.[192] And, in a fresher vein, the paragraph about the sleeping infant Isobel, 'like some losthappy leaf', is a delicate lyric that suggests Hopkins's 'Spring and Fall'.[556]

On the whole, there were not many obstacles to keep Swift from living up to his definition of style: 'proper words in proper places'. The wear and tear on language since his time, the corruptions of usage, the vulgarizations of journalism, the affectations of scholarship, have so relaxed the standard that we are no longer surprised to find proper words in improper places. Joyce, with Swift's feeling for linguistic elegance and sense of outraged propriety, has a very different language to handle; the style of *Finnegans Wake*, which shocks us into an awareness of the difference, may be defined as 'improper words in proper places'. Joyce utilizes the malapropism as the literary expression of social maladjustment, the language of the outlaw. The boyish inscription in a closet of Clongowes Wood College, *Julius Caesar wrote the Calico Belly*, was more than a reduction to absurdity; it was a protest against things as they are. But the genius of Mrs. Malaprop offers a means of escape, as well as a mode of criticism, and sometimes casts a temporary glamour over familiar things. Joyce revised the nursery rhyme, 'Ride a cock horse', to advertise 'Anna Livia Plurabelle'. The one quality she had in common with the fine lady was music, so that is the one word of the last line that does not undergo a sea-change: *Sheashell ebb music wayriver she flows.*

Portmanteau-words and malapropisms can be isolated and analysed; heavier luggage and longer passages are more securely embedded in the text. When every word of a simple declarative sentence is subjected to the same sort of alteration, the result is not too complex. 'Nobirdy aviar soar anywing to eagle it' is simply an ornithological fashion of stating that nobody ever saw anything to equal it.[505] Most of Joyce's sentences are acted upon by more complicating forces. The result is a polyphonic phrasing which takes its key from its most consistent combination of sounds and meanings, but may be modified by substitution or addition at any point. One of the simplest questions of the book is 'How hominous his house, haunt it?'[560] Here the subdominant would be 'How ominous his house, ain't it?' The tonic, through the allusive and alliterative influence of the keyword, 'house', has introduced 'home' and 'haunt'. The dominant augments the chord by bringing out the latinate adjective for humanity and shifting the question to an injunction. There is a further consonance between 'ominous' and 'haunt', and between the whole sentence and the main theme. In comparison with the contrapuntal possibilities of this way of writing, the Siren scene from *Ulysses* is plainsong.

Another instance, more strictly measured, is a line from Shaun's account of the Gracehoper's despair: 'Was he come to hevre with his engiles or gone to hull with the poop?'[416] Here the honours seem fairly divided between crossing the North Sea and finding out someone's destination in the next world. Not quite fairly. 'Hevre' is equally Havre and heaven, as 'engiles' refers impartially to the ship's engines and God's angels; but hell hides behind the redoubled opacity of Hull, and 'poop' is literal because of the blasphemous suggestion about the Pope. Since the answer to the equation is already hinted by the symmetrical relationship of both parts of the two clauses, no meaning is lost by the displacement, and a certain emphasis is gained. Every sentence is a wilful divagation from the expectations raised by the last. While the rhythmic undercurrent is pulling us in one direction, the drift of associations carries us the other way. By listening carefully, we can make out a number of recurrent lilts and metrical patterns, pulsating through the fluctuations of verbalism. Bear in mind this concise formulation of Vico's doctrine:[215]

Teems of times and happy returns. The seim anew.

The children's hour is responsible for a variation:[277]

We drames our dreams tell Bappy returns. And Sein annews.

The *Götterdämmerung* has a terrifying effect on the words, and leaves the tune unchanged:[510]

—Booms of bombs and heavy rethudders?
—This aim to you!

By the time the Phoenix arises, it is an old story, and we are ready
—as in the song about Old Man Finnegan—to begin again:[614]

Themes have thimes and habit reburns. To flame in you.

The system of *leitmotif* borrows more heavily from literary
echoes than *Ulysses*, although the cadences of nature are a crucial
exception. Rain has its own distinctive rhythm, which adapts itself
to an impression of Earwicker's drunken discomfort, as he tosses
about at the end of an episode:[74]

Liverpoor? Sot a bit of it! His braynes coolt parritch, his pelt nassy,
his heart's adrone, his bluidstreams acrawl, his puff but a piff, his
extremities extremely so.

Later on, when deeper slumber has made him deaf to the rain, he
is personified as a bridge crossing Dublin Bay:[266]

Rivapool? Hod a brieck on it! But its piers eerie, its span spooky, its toll
but a till, its parapets all peripateting.

The 'hitherandthithering waters of' the Liffey are presented with
endless versatility;[265] Earwicker is represented by the incremental
repetition of 'The House that Jack Built'.[511] 'John Peel', as a
drinking song, owes its authority to a hunting print on display at
the Bristol.[31] There are doubtless a number of signs advertising
Guinness's stout. The ubiquitous slogan is broadcast on the final
day: hustled from your graves, when the conquering hero appears
in triumph, you are informed that 'genghis is ghoon for you'.[593]
The noble motto of the Order of the Garter is quoted,[113] only to be
flouted,[495] and the Lord's Prayer is taken in vain by Kate, the cross-
grained housemaid, with searing Joycean blasphemy.[530] Joyce, in
his echolalia, is revisited by fragments and reminiscences so profusely scattered and so deeply charged, that his maltreatment of
them is a culminating gesture of dissent from a lifelong disciple of
the fallen archangel. His work is a gargantuan burlesque, not of
any other given work, but of the entire cultural heritage.

Often his allusions to other writers justify themselves by en-
livening a trite refrain: 'Walhalloo, Walhalloo, Walhalloo, mourn

in plein!' is a manifest improvement upon Victor Hugo's '*Waterloo, Waterloo, Waterloo, morne plaine!*'[541] On the Belgian battlefield, which it lets you keep in sight, it heaps Valhalla, a war cry, full mourning, and full morning. Joyce is not afraid to hinge the critical point of an episode on an elusive reference. He sketches out the setting for Earwicker's downfall, without mentioning the arsenal, by parodying an epigram that Swift wrote when it was built:

> Behold a proof of Irish sense,
> Here Irish wit is seen!
> Where nothing's left that's worth defence,
> They build a magazine!

Joyce falls short of the biting Anglophobia of his model, though he touches, somewhat self-consciously, on Swift's visit to England in the matter of tithes: 'Behove this sound of Irish sense. Really? Here English might be seen. Royally? One sovereign punned to petery pence. Regally? The silence speaks the scene. Fake!'[12] The nearer Joyce comes to a scene or an emotion, the more prone he is to indulge in literary by-play. When Earwicker's *cri du coeur* is muffled in a travesty of *Macbeth*, we may assume a studied evasion on the author's part, a determination to detach himself from his characters at all costs: 'For a burning would is come to dance inane. Glamours hath moidered's lieb and herefore Coldours must leap no more. Lack breath must leap no more.'[250]

These distractions are quite deliberate. If Earwicker's plight really held our attention and solicitude, we should consider them heartless, far-fetched, and even cheap. Joyce shows no more concern for his hero than a geneticist for a fruit-fly; he happens to be interested in the peculiarities of the *genus* earwig. Indifferent, he pares his fingernails, having reached the stage of artistic development that passes over the individual in favour of the general. The divine, far-off event toward which Joyce's doomsday book moves is a 'general election'.[253] By associating ideas and multiplying parallels he is attempting to universalize his limited subject-matter. Universality, in so far as he can be said to have attained it, is a mosaic of particulars. When he reverts to basic situations, primary emotions, and final values, he is willing to take them for granted. His serious interest is focused on the manifold permutations of shape, colour—in the last analysis—language. Of the romance between his hero and heroine he has a good deal to say, but no more to express than the schoolboy who carves 'HCE loves ALP' on a tree-trunk. Instead of selecting the *mot juste*, Joyce acccumulates a Rabelaisian catalogue of epithets: '. . . neoliffic smith and magdalenian jinnyjones . . . martial sin with peccadilly . . . solomn one and shebby . . . Regies Producer with screendoll Vedette'.[576]

Here the characters, grotesquely magnified and romantically draped, are lay figures. The real romance is between Joyce and the language. Even when his subject is moribund, his writing is alive. The result of his experiments fits in surprisingly well with the conclusions toward which critical theories and poetic practice, propaganda studies and pedagogical tests, semantics and logical positivism, have lately been pushing us. We used to lament that words were such a shadowy approximation of objective reality. We have learned to look upon them as objects of immediate apprehension, more real in themselves than their penumbras of meaning. They were always symbols, to be sure, but we had fallen into the careless habit of confounding the symbol with its referents. Joyce, conceding the priority of the word to the thing, renews our perception of language as an artistic medium. When he sought words, in the hospital chapter of *Ulysses*, to reproduce the origins of life, he was foiled by the intervention of literary history, embryology, and other excrescences. Turning from representation to presentation, he allows nothing to intervene between the prose of *Finnegans Wake* and the flow of the Liffey.

Joyce's book, with more reason that Jules Romains' interminable pot-boiler, is describable as a *roman-fleuve*. Its most authentic voice is the prosopopoeia of the river, rippling upwards to the surface of consciousness in all her feminine moods and changes. When Anna Livia is introduced, she is a vivacious young girl in a shower of spring rain: 'Arrah, sure, we all love little Anny Ruiny, or, we mean to say, lovelittle Anna Rayiny, when unda her brella, mid piddle med puddle she ninnygoes nannygoes nancing by.'[7]

Later she makes a mature appearance, conveying words of maternal comfort to the feckless Shem, 'babbling, bubbling, chattering to herself, deloothering the fields on their elbows leaning with the sloothering slide of her, giddgaddy, grannyma, gossipaceous Anna Livia'.[195] By the end her remembrance of girlhood ('just a young thin pale soft shy slim slip of a thing'[202]) has been transferred to her daughter *con variazioni* ('just a whisk brisk sly spry spink spank sprint of a thing'[627]). A shower, a stream, a freshet, the river rises until it drowns out the other sounds. Meanwhile, on the banks of the Liffey, two old washerwomen gossip about Earwicker and his family, proceeding 'to make his private linen public' until nightfall has transformed them into a tree and a stone:[215]

Can't hear with the waters of. The chittering waters of. Flittering bats, fieldmice bawk talk. Ho! Are you not gone ahome? What Thom Malone? Can't hear with bawk of bats, all thim liffeying waters of. Ho, talk save us! My foos won't moos. I feel as old as yonder elm. A tale told of Shaun or Shem? All Livia's daughtersons. Dark hawks hear us. Night! Night! My ho head halls. I feel as heavy as yonder stone. Tell me of John or Shaun? Who were Shem and Shaun the living sons or daughters of? Night now! Tell me, tell me, tell me, elm! Night night! Telmetale of stem or stone. Beside the rivering waters of, hitherand-thithering waters of. Night!

This paragraph, the last of the first section, is among the few that yielded to a committee of seven French translators, collaborating with Joyce. Their task, like Urquhart's with Rabelais, was to translate a style—*double-entendre* for pun, '*le parc de l'Inphernix*' for 'the Fiendish Park'—where a literal translation would have been meaningless. They proved, at all events, that the application of Joyce's technique is not restricted to English. Assonance is easier in French, and orthography is harder:

*N'entends pas cause les ondes de. Le bébé babil des ondes de. Souris chauve, trottinette cause pause. Hein! Tu n'es pas rentré? Quel père André N'entends pas cause les fuisouris, les liffeyantes ondes de. Eh! Bruit nous aide! Mon pied à pied se lie lierré. Je me sens vieille comme mon orme même. Un conte conté de Shaun ou Shem? De Livie tous les fillefils. Sombre faucons écoutent l'ombre. Nuit. Nuit. Ma taute tête tombe. Je me sens lourde comme ma pierrestone. Conte moi de John ou Shaun. Qui furent*

*Shem et Shaun en vie les fils ou filles de. Là-dessus nuit. Dis-mor, dis-mor, dis-mor, orme. Nuit, nuit! Contemoiconte soit tronc ou pierre. Tant rivierantes ondes de, couretcourantes ondes de. Nuit.*

Difficulties of the opposite kind were met by C. K. Ogden, when he turned the same passage into Basic English, as an accompaniment to Joyce's recording. His problem was not to imitate the suggestiveness of the original, but to reduce it to direct statement. Hence he is forced to ignore harmonies and conceits, and to rule out ambiguities, sometimes rather arbitrarily. There is not much left:

No sound but the waters of. The dancing waters of. Winged things in flight, field-rats louder than talk. Ho! Are you not gone, ho! What Tom Malone? No sound but the noise of these things, the Liffey and all its waters of. Ho, talk safe keep us! There's no moving this my foot. I seem as old as that tree over there. A story of Shaun or Shem but where? All Livia's daughters and sons. Dark birds are hearing. Night! Night! My old head's bent. My weight is like that stone you see. What may the John Shaun story be? Or who were Shem and Shaun the living sons and daughters of? Night now! Say it, say it, tree! Night night! The story say of stem or stone. By the side of the river waters of, this way and that way waters of. Night!

This self-denying paraphrase juxtaposes the simplest and the most complex English, Mr. Ogden's language of strict denotation and Joyce's language of extreme connotation. Both are reactions against our modern Babel, and Mr. Ogden has hailed Joyce as 'the bellwether of debabelization'. While his enemies have attacked him for conducting a campaign to disintegrate literature, his friends have rallied to 'the revolution of the word'. In sober fact, Joyce is neither an obscurantist nor a logodedalist, neither a destroyer nor a creator of language. He could scarcely achieve his microscopic precision and polysemantic subtlety unless he were a neutral. His restless play of allusion depends, to the vast extent of his knowledge, on the acceptance of a linguistic *status quo*. Within his top-heavy frame of reference, everything must be in its place. Whatever is capable of being sounded or enunciated will find its echo in *Finnegans Wake*: Joyce alludes glibly and impartially to such concerns as left-wing literature,[116] Whitman and democracy,[263]

Lenin and Marxism,[271] the Gestapo,[332] the Nazis,[375] the Soviets,[414] and the 'braintrust'.[529] The sounds are heard, the names called, the phrases invoked, as it were by a well-informed parrot. The rest is 'SILENCE'.[501]

Perhaps this is what T. S. Eliot had in mind when he cited Joyce as the most orthodox writer of our time. Like the artisans of the medieval cathedrals, he uses available symbols and deductive methods to mirror a comprehensive world in a difficult medium. Like his own description of the Vatican, his book is a museum, 'chalkfull of masterplasters'.[152] Compounded of so many tales and legends that have fascinated mankind, it has no story to tell. It does not narrate; it elaborates; it projects a poignant series of cross-references. Again, permanently this time, a warm flux of material is resolved into cold and stationary thought. Wyndham Lewis was rash enough to cite *Ulysses* as an example of our morbid 'time-consciousness', and Joyce has stuck his tongue out at Lewis in *Finnegans Wake*.[292] It was Joyce's lifelong endeavour, when all is said and done, to escape from the nightmare of history, to conceive the totality of human experience on a simultaneous plane, to synchronize past, present, and future in the timelessness of a millennium. Time is spatialized, a mere auxiliary to the other three dimensions. Space is curved, boundless and finite, the same anew. The Ondt, 'making spaces in his psyche',[416] exults over the Gracehoper.

Yet it is a waste of time to command the waves to stand still, and the river—despite the frantic cries of 'Stop! Please stop!'—is never stagnant. In spite of what we have repeatedly noted, that Joyce's art is static, nature remains fluid. Tolstoy had a keener perception of the disparities between civilization and nature: between the *comme il faut* of Petersburg and the folkways of the Cossacks, the mincing gestures of Napoleon and the motherwit of the Russian peasant, the war of 1812 and the comet of 1812. But Joyce, while he narrows civilization down to art, is always ready to give nature her due. His 'ecotaph' is as dead as Saint Peter's rock; his 'livetree' is always fertile.[420] His words are the living part of his work, because they must spring organically from human intercourse before they can be mechanically controlled by personal artifice. He can invent many compounds, but he cannot synthetize language, since the *logos* is the one thing that existed in the beginning. He can only murmur, with Victor Hugo, '*Le mot c'est le Verbe et le Verbe c'est Dieu!*' He has no trouble in believing, with Max Müller and his school, that language animates myth. In our attempts to follow Joyce's associative logic and to sample his overwhelming detail, we may have lost sight of the symmetry of his design. By stripping his largest abstractions of everything except their relationship, we can review in a glance the elements of his work and their theoretical substructure:

| The Language of the Outlaw | The Nightmare of History |
|---|---|
| LANGUAGE | MYTH |
| NATURE | ART |
| RIVER (Liffey) | CITY (Dublin) |

TREE-STONE (Isolde: Tristan)

| FEMALE (ALP: Shem) | MALE (HCE: Shaun) |
|---|---|
| MATTER | FORM |
| TIME | SPACE |
| Bruno's System of Metaphysics | Vico's Philosophy of History |

The parallel columns could be ramified indefinitely, or else they could be simplified to two monosyllables—life and death. For Joyce is finally taking his leave of the monumental ruins of the city of man, and attaching his hope to the matriarchal continuity of the years, the seasons, and the months. The dogmas and manifestoes of the Mookse and the Gripes, the orthodoxies and iconoclasms of the Pope and the Patriarch, collapse into heaps of dirty linen on the banks of the Liffey. The damp twilight falls, obliterating the rights and wrongs of man-made controversy. 'Reeve Gootch was right and Reeve Drughad was sinistrous!'[197] It hardly matters any more, whether the *Rive Gauche* or the Right Bank was farther to the left. What matters is the river that still flows between them. In the last pages of *Finnegans Wake*, as in *Ulysses*, the citizen has sunk into dreamless sleep, 'adamant evar'.[626] Earwicker's worries, at their perihelion, are of bankruptcy—our last news of the progress of civilization.[589] The female epilogue commences in the rustling of leaves on a tree, continues in the clouds and the rain, and pours forth with the river into the bay and out to sea, on the impetus of a homing instinct or a death-wish.[619] The wooded peninsula of Howth stirs the same recollection in Annie as in Molly Bloom: 'There's where. First.'[628] The final image is Bloom's lone symbol for poetry, a gull over the waters. The final situation is that of Stephen's bird-like vision, when, walking along the shore and looking northward toward Howth, he first felt the ecstasy of flight and discovered himself to be an artist.

A new beginning, a rebirth, spring again, morning once more. The mother, Mrs. Mooney, has passed out with the tide; long live the cloud-girl daughter, 'let her rain'.[627] Erect and threatening, the giant has been overcome by twin Titans, and the Titans will be overcome by stranger gods. Meanwhile, his expiring orgasm is a foretaste of death: H. C. Earwicker is 'rehearsing somewan's funeral'.[477] It could be anyone's, just as the rites of Tammuz or Osiris, Attis or Adonis, could enact the burial and regeneration of many peoples and of the earth itself. Joyce's funeral games adhere to the established ritual of numberless terrestrial myths, so ancient and universal that Sir James Frazer could compile twelve volumes of them to show how myth is intertwined with the roots of religion. Among modern nations, the Irish are noted for the hearty good cheer with which they celebrate death; but 'wake', in the brogue, has the additional meaning of 'week'. And that signifies one particular week, combining, for Irish Catholics, the celebration of the profoundest mystery of their religion with the most stirring event in the recent history of their country. Easter is the Christian ceremony of resurrection. Easter Week, 1916, was the occasion of the bloody uprising that foreshadowed the resurgence of the Irish Free State.

To Joyce, wildgoose though he was, these climaxes of religious and nationalistic emotion had a compelling force that his great refusal and his unregenerate internationalism could twist and strain, but never weaken. Disgruntlement had taught him the art of sinking, so that he could, and did, subvert them into anticlimaxes. But his maudlin mockery is an act of possession as well as an exorcism; in a single subversive operation, he can embrace and deride the same words, slogans, sentiments, or ideologies. What was his attitude toward the eulogy of Parnell in 'Ivy Day in the Committee Room'? The question which ushers in Joyce's definitive self-portrait is a ribald parody of a sentimental poem by Thomas Campbell, 'Exile of Erin'. When Joyce, the 'acheseyeld from Ailing', guffaws with a whimper, he is describing his own ambivalence.[148] Beneath the convulsive guffaws of *Finnegans Wake*, we can hear the whimpering of Campbell's lines:

> *Erin, my country! Though sad and forsaken,*
> *In dreams I revisit thy sea-beaten shore;*
> *But, alas! in a far foreign land I awaken,*
> *And sigh for the friends who can meet me no more!*

Campbell, not irrelevantly, was a Scotchman. In adapting his vicarious sentimentality, Joyce too keeps returning to 'the bold anthem of Erin go bragh' ('Ireland forever'). He sings out, with a vainglorious note of Germanic aggressiveness, 'For Ehren, boys, gobrawl'.[338] He hums snatches of genuine Irish melody from the romantic poets—Moore's 'At the mid hour of night',[328] Mangan's 'Dark Rosaleen'.[351] To his letter, or to his book, 'written in smoke and blurred by mist and signed of solitude',[337] he knows there is an obvious reply, a telegram, variously worded, always bearing the same message: 'Come back to old Erin'.[421] He still prefers the view from Pisgah. In his book, in all his books, he does go back to the promised land. *Finnegans Wake* is a voluble and lusty retort to the premature lament of Yeats:

> *Romantic Ireland's dead and gone,*
> *It's with O'Leary in the grave.*

Joyce's book of the dead calls upon the O'Learys and the Finnegans and all good Irishmen to awake and come forth by day. 'Irise, Osirises!'[493] Persse O'Reilly performs the part of a culture hero, with the recognition that two of the victims of the Easter massacre were named Pearse and O'Rahilly. The O'Rahilly was shot down in the streets, but Pearse was imprisoned, with a number of the Sinn Fein leaders, at Kilmainhan. When they were taken away to be executed, someone chalked on the walls of the prison, which had looked down on Emmet and O'Connell and Parnell, 'We shall rise again'. One of the bloodiest conflicts was fought before Joyce's college, on Stephen's Green, and his collaborator in the undergraduate pamphlet containing 'The Day of the Rabblement', Sheehy-Skeffington, was one of those killed. Joyce, who had paid his final visit to Ireland four years before, has his alibi for not having engaged in sporting matches with the black and tans.[176] He had to wait for the newspapers to find out about the executions, 'with them newnesboys pearcin screaming off their armsworths'. It is his prophecy that Patrick Pearse and Sir Roger Casement—disguised, by German intrigue, as 'Deductive Almayne Rogers'—and the other Fenians cannot be kept down. One after the other, to the rousing music of 'Old Man River', the Irish heroes will rise from their graves: 'Heat wives rasing. They jest keeps rosing. He jumps leaps rizing. How long!'[363]

The link between their resurrection and that of Jesus—the last link in our concatenation of thought—is 'the rann, the rann, that keen of old bards', which connects this passage with the elevation of the host during the ballad of Persse O'Reilly.[46] A rann is an old saying, but Joyce is concerned with an older custom, the hunting of the wren. Irish boys, according to Frazer, kill a wren on Christmas; on the following day, Stephen's own name-day, they hoist it on a broomstick, garnished with holly and ivy, and march from house to house, chanting:

> *The wren, the wren, the king of all birds,*
> *St. Stephen's Day was caught in the furze;*
> *Although he is little, his family's great,*
> *I pray you, good landlady, give us a treat.*

Although a wren is as insignificant a scapegoat as you could choose, his family includes kings and priests, dying gods and sleeping heroes. And his sacrifice will serve, as well as another's, to ensure the continued round of life. The cycle of history is propelled by revolutions, the years and months are the cause and the effect of decay, and the week-end is the microcosm of the end of the world. 'After suns and moons, dews and wettings, thunders and fires, comes sabotag'.[409] Destruction, decadence, and death are the pre-conditions of fertility. When we face the chaos that individualism has made of our world, we accept the unrelenting conclusion that individuals must be sacrificed, if there is ever to be another cosmos. 'Except a grain of wheat fall into the earth and die, it abideth by itself alone,' says the gospel of Saint John, 'but if it die, it beareth much fruit.' A hard saying, but not a hopeless one. It is not only the burden of the manifold texts of *Finnegans Wake*; it is, explicitly or implicitly, the text which the most serious and percipient of modern writers have expounded with an ever-increasing urgency—Dostoevsky in *The Brothers Karamazov*, Tolstoy in *Resurrection*, Ibsen in *When We Dead Awaken*, Zola in *Le Débâcle*, Gide in *Si le grain ne meurt*, Eliot in *The Waste Land*, and Mann in his *Joseph* tetralogy.

# 3. Richness

At the opening of the twentieth century, Anatole France, scanning the horizons of European culture, discerned two vast cities, the works of Tolstoy and Zola. His metaphor was aptly chosen for that powerful generation of naturalistic novelists, which was disappearing even as Synge was demanding that richness be united to reality. The evolution of realism, since the medieval burghers preferred their crude *fabliaux* to the idealized romances of chivalry, has been the growth of the city. In painting, earlier than in fiction, prosperous citizens of free Flemish towns discovered that art, instead of symbolizing the ideals of their religion, could mirror the fullness of their lives. But, for a number of reasons, both sociological and technological, the novel has become perhaps the most characteristic form of art in our bourgeois civilization. And naturalism has been the prevailing tendency of the novel—until very recently. The inference should be clear. Under the increasing pressures of capitalism, the petty *bourgeoisie* is bound to present a dismal picture of triviality and frustration. Joyce's books, he was proud to admit, are devoted to the destinies of members of the lower middle class—to the economic decline of the Dedalus family, to Bloom's future on the dole, to Earwicker's bankruptcy.

As his subject-matter reveals the decomposition of the middle class, Joyce's technique passes beyond the limits of realistic fiction. Neither the *Portrait of the Artist* nor *Finnegans Wake* is a novel, strictly speaking, and *Ulysses* is a novel to end all novels. When it was published, Richard Aldington, in some alarm, took it to be 'the gravestone, the cromlech of naturalism'. T. S. Eliot was prepared to face the consequences of this view, and to inquire whether the novel had not outlived its function since Flaubert and James, and whether *Ulysses* should not be considered an epic. In the *Dial*, which had just awarded him its annual poetry prize for *The Waste Land*, Eliot went on to make this prescient comment on the significance of Joyce's method:

In using the myth, in manipulating a continuous parallel between contemporaneity and antiquity, Mr. Joyce is pursuing a method which others must pursue after him. They will not be imitators, any more than the scientist who uses the discoveries of an Einstein in pursuing his own, independent, further investigations. It is simply a way of controlling, of ordering, of giving a shape and a significance to the immense panorama of futility and anarchy which is contemporary history. It is a method already adumbrated by Mr. Yeats, and of the need for which I believe Mr. Yeats to have been the first contemporary to be conscious. It is, I seriously believe, a step toward making the modern world possible in art.

Eliot's review, 'Ulysses, Order, and Myth', provides the answer to Aldington's argument that *Ulysses* is 'an invitation to chaos'— an argument that had been seconded by the majority of Joyce's critics and capped by *The Dublin Review*, with Shane Leslie's *ex cathedra* charge of 'literary bolshevism'. It is the common experience of proponents of a new order to be denounced as anarchists. 'Since you can draw so beautifully, why do you spend your time making those queer things?' someone asked Pablo Picasso. 'That's the reason,' he replied. Joyce, to a similar question from Frank Budgen, responded that it would have been easy to turn out two conventional books every year, but that it would not have been worth doing. The high standard of competent mediocrity that characterizes the arts, in an epoch of museums and machines, makes it too easy to express oneself and too difficult to say anything new. Originality is dearly bought by a ruthless determination to cut through *clichés*. The creative artist, Joyce or Picasso, Eliot or Stravinsky, must be coldly and deliberately exceptional. He must not only surpass his predecessors; he must surpass himself. Hence those accelerated developments that compel him to go from climax to climax, bringing forth every few years a new style and another revelation.

It is not surprising that twentieth-century literature is diagnosed as *Kulturbolschewismus*, or that literary experiments are condemned as personal eccentricities. The valuable contribution of Edmund Wilson, when he brought out *Axel's Castle* ten years ago, was his informed interpretation of six of our most original contemporary writers, including Joyce, and his clear-sighted perception—beyond their idiosyncratic works—of the outlines of a movement. So much has happened during those ten years, that it is not Mr. Wilson's fault if his book failed to sense the direction of that movement. Starting from the rather inadequate definition of symbolism that Arthur Symons took over from the *symbolistes*, he was unprepared to carry his analysis much further than the last gasp of romanticism. His conclusions posited the need for a stronger sense of social responsibility, and seemed to suggest that it could be met by reversion to some naïver plane of naturalism. But the experience of the past decade, particularly with the *ersatz* product known as 'socialist realism', must have disillusioned him. On the other hand, if we concluded—with Mr. Wilson—that symbolism was dying out, we are now witnesses to the unmistakable fact that it has as many lives as the late Tim Finnegan. Though it is by nature an experimental and transitional phase, some important results have lately been coming out of the laboratory.

Our miscalculations were based on the assumption that symbolism is more individualistic than naturalism. The contrary, we are beginning to see, is nearer the truth. The whole dilemma of modern literature, and of modern society, has been most sharply evident in America, and has been summed up by Walt Whitman in the first two lines of *Leaves of Grass*:

> *One's self I sing, a simple separate person,*
> *Yet utter the word Democratic, the word En-Masse.*

The novel, from Defoe to Proust, has been a chronicle of separate —though not always simple—existences, reflecting the ruggedness and decadence of individual enterprise. The industrial revolution, along with such confusing words as 'democratic' and *'en masse'*, forced a hard choice upon novelists: protest or escape. The social protest of the realists—whether of a Catholic like Balzac or a radical like Dickens—is still an exercise of individualism, since it is able to stand apart and attack the shortcomings of a *laissez-faire* society. It has, of course, more ethical justification than the manœuvres of symbolists like Poe or Huysmans, seeking to escape into their own lurid imaginations. But psychologists can show that there is no escape, and that such introspection is actually a sensitive gauge of external forces. Many of our most subjective writers, without reversing their course, have found within themselves the keys to a broader objectivity. They have found themselves consciously moving from the slippery regions of psychology to the *terra firma* of anthropology. They have learned that the infancy of the human race is recapitulated in the infancy of the individual, and that myths are collective dreams. Science, it seems, is on the side of symbolism, after all.

If Zola, the pseudo-scientific spokesman of the naturalistic school, is remembered, it will not be for his exploded hypotheses and questionable documentation, but for the Rodinesque energy with which he symbolizes issues. In *La faute de l'abbé Mouret*, the fall of a young priest takes place in a kind of paradise, the garden of Paradou; in *Germinal*, the smouldering mine of Tartaret is another Tartarus, where chained Titans are kept down; in the glamorous role of Aphrodite, the courtesan *Nana* is introduced on a full stage. Today's revival of poetic drama should remind us that the theatre has been at best an imperfect medium for naturalism, and has always leaned heavily upon symbolism for its most striking effects. The dramatic gesture of Ibsen's Nora, when she dances the tarantella and slams the door, was a ritual of deliverance for nineteenth-century womanhood. At the opposite pole, it was the symbolist Melville, adjuring society for solitude, who had the fullest measure of success in creating the American epic. And it was the arch-symbolist Wagner who—out of romantic vagaries and theatrical makeshifts and brilliant orchestration—forged the uncreated conscience of the Third Reich. The theory of Marx's renegade disciple, Georges Sorel, that political ideologies are simply modern variants of the myth, has been cogently demonstrated. In the oracular phrase of Paul Valéry, '*Songez que demain est un mythe. . . .*'

Recent scholarship and critical appreciation, culminating in F. O. Matthiessen's *American Renaissance*, have made available our own heritage of moral allegory from Hawthorne through James. From the continent, the posthumous influence of Franz Kafka, a Jew whose home was Prague and whose language was German, has cast its visionary glow over the work of many young writers. André Malraux, like Ernest Hemingway, has been journeying across the world, searching for adventures large enough to exalt the modern intellectual into a tragic hero. If John Steinbeck stands out from the other American local colourists, it is because of the legendary proportions of his theme. The most impressive novelist of Soviet Russia, Mikhail Sholokhov, has vigorously continued the epic strain of Tolstoy. Ignazio Silone, exiled to Switzerland, has converted Italian folk-tales into anti-Fascist fables. The most significant example of all, and—since Joyce's death—the unchallenged master of living novelists, is Thomas Mann. Mann is a more typical and explicit figure than Joyce, possibly because he has worked in a narrower and heavier tradition. He has been exiled by fascism, not by philistinism. In many respects he has remained, as he once told fellow-citizens of his native Lübeck, '*ein bürgerlicher Erzähler*'. His development has proceeded, in the phrase of his lecture on Freud, 'from the bourgeois and individual to the typical and mythical'.

Mann's itinerary conforms so closely to Joyce's progression from naturalism to symbolism that it brings home to us the historical necessities that have moulded their widely separated careers. The first stage, *Bürgertum*, is commemorated by Mann's substantial novel of a declining family in a decaying Hanseatic municipality, *Buddenbrooks*, while Joyce's early impressions of his city are sketched in *Dubliners*. Significantly, Joyce's first major effort was the *Portrait of the Artist*, while Mann's stage of *Künstlertum* produced mainly sketches and *novellen* in which the wandering artist, *ein verrirter Bürger*, from Schiller to Gustav von Aschenbach, deplores his inability to enjoy the delights of the commonplace.

The post-war years conferred *Weltbürgertum* upon Mann, and saw the completion of his synthesis of the European mind, *Der Zauberberg*. Since this pivotal work—brought down, like *Ulysses*, from the neutral Alps—he has abandoned the teachings of the authoritarian Naphta for the liberal humanism of his Settembrini. His work in progress, in a very different way from *Finnegans Wake*, descends through the deep well of the past to the same timeless and timely theme. The story of Joseph, with his many-coloured coat and his prophetic dreams, is not merely another apologue of the artist, but of the fate of culture itself, sold into slavery in Egypt:

For it *is*, always *is*, however much we may say It was. Thus speaks the myth, which is only the garment of the mystery. But the holiday garment of the mystery is the feast, the recurrent feast which bestrides the tenses and makes the has-been and the to-be present to the popular sense. What wonder then, that on the day of the feast humanity is in a ferment and conducts itself with licensed abandon? For in it life and death meet and know each other. Feast of story-telling, thou are the festal garment of life's mystery, for thou conjurest up timelessness in the mind of the folk, and invokest the myth that it may be relived in the actual present.

In fear and trembling, we pay belated homage to the idols of the tribe. In the paintings of Picasso's negro period or Stravinsky's *Sacre du printemps* we recognize the fructifying resources of primitivism, and we feel its destructive menace in the headlines of the morning papers. Marx predicted that mythology, the relic of a primitive state, would disappear as soon as we had mastered nature; but we are farther than ever from the mastery of human nature. The myth by itself is neither good nor bad. Its worth—as Hitler taught Mann—depends on the feast. Without that communal basis, life is isolated by the drab disorders of urban civilization, and art can only formulate private mythologies. Where there is a community, there is an integration: art has a function, life a pattern. Symbolism bears its true fruit when men are joined together in an imaginative order, and their daily behaviour is invested with a ceremonial dignity. The myth-maker submerges the self in the mass; the artist is a burgher gone astray. The novel is a production and a condemnation of the city. The myth is an expression and a celebration of the community.

Further speculation would be utopian. We still live—with an uneasy glance toward the sky—in cities, and our would-be myth-makers are still artists. Seen from any historical perspective, it is the distinguishing characteristic of the modern writer that he should consider himself a practitioner of the fine arts. In the eighteenth century, the man of letters was *par excellence* a critic. Whenever we think of Voltaire, Johnson, or Lessing, we think of criticism, though they practised the diverse *genres* of their day. Theirs was a day of accepted standards, and they could criticize with the assurance that their criteria would be known and respected. Values had so shifted, by the nineteenth century, that they could no longer be taken for granted. And so the critic became a prophet, and exhausted his artistic efforts in promulgating some pet dogma or peculiar message. A novelist, like Dostoevsky, or a dramatist, like Ibsen, was hailed as a saviour or damned as a charlatan. A poet, like Victor Hugo, was a *mage effaré*. Consequently, rather than trouble with form, the most influential writers set up as lay preachers—Carlyle, Emerson, Nietzsche.

But society has a way of disregarding prophets, and writers have a way of abandoning their plans for saving society. In their dis-affection, they rushed to the other extreme. The cult of art for art's sake arose, as the Marxist critic Plekhanov shrewdly observed, when discord had developed between the writer and his environment. Théophile Gautier shouted from the housetops his discovery that the bust survives the city. Flaubert shut himself up in the provinces, declaring that—to be an artist—a man must be willing to give up fatherland, religion, and social conviction. Joyce, on his departure from Ireland, might have been echoing this negative credo. In positive devotion to his self-imposed labours, with all the earnestness of a religion and all the playfulness of a game, he carried the discipline and the indulgence of art to greater lengths than any writer had done before or was likely to do again. He lived his work and he wrote his life. The self-portrait of Icarus-Dædalus is the *livre vécu* of the martyred artist.

Elaborating his life-work in silence and cunning, Joyce must have been conscious of the stature he was assuming as a proscribed symbol of the European man of letters in the twentieth century. He must have relished the irony of circumstance that made his work a portentous contribution to the literature of a country which he had always distrusted, and which had returned the compliment. English fiction, since Hardy renounced it, has had an undistinguished record. It has had the facile competence of the Bennetts and Galsworthys; it has had the febrile energy of D. H. Lawrence and the bloodless grace of Virginia Woolf. Its distinction has been borrowed from three outsiders—the American, James; the Pole, Conrad; and the Irishman, Joyce. Joyce is never more of a fighting Irishman than in his attitude toward the British Empire. Something of his own country's unremitting feud has been transferred to his own relations with his country. Sinn Fein means 'ourselves alone'. Joyce, holding out against the world, *unus contra mundum*, is a one-man Sinn Fein movement. Alone, he keeps returning to the doorstep of Stephen Dedalus. In the *Portrait of the Artist*, the city was transfigured by his reading; in *Finnegans Wake*, cosmopolitan literary *pastiche* is flavoured by recollections of parochial Dublin.

By virtue of his very isolation, as a Parisian Irishman and a heretical Catholic, he has become a type, expatriate and excommunicate, the man without a country and without a belief. We have scarcely been able to examine a single aspect of his writing without spying the shadow of his religious background. Catholicism endowed him with a personal relation to the Mediterranean past. His exclusion from the Catholic communion—and here, surely, we may play upon words—fostered his unwillingness to communicate. The effect of his blindness on his incomparable ear, or on his poetic gifts, we cannot estimate; but we may be sure that it deepened the soul's incurable loneliness, and made him feel the same calling which had prompted Milton, in darkness, danger, and solitude, to write of chaos and night. Limitations become virtues in the performance of this function: his characterization is static because his characters are paralysed. The mechanical ingenuity of his technique is a fit vehicle for the literature of a scientific age. The encrustation of literary learning, with which he covers up his emotional evasions, is an appropriately Alexandrian touch. When we condemn Joyce, we are condemning ourselves.

He will doubtless go down in the histories of literature as the archetype of misunderstood genius. If we could eliminate the causes of misunderstanding, by some process of critical chemistry, we should find that his genius was far happier—far less tragic and far more humorous—than the brooding morbidity of his books would indicate. The motley of a Rabelais, under happier circumstances, would have sat more comfortably upon him. The *saeva indignatio* was a reaction to his age; the *vis comica* was his natural bent. With his mind so divided against itself, so full of unshared emotions, he inevitably hit upon the formula of Renan—irony and pity. These are both admirable qualities, but we may observe that the writers who cultivate them have seldom succeeded in combining them: they lavish the irony on the world and save the pity for themselves. The result is the wavering tone of the *Portrait of the Artist* and even *Ulysses*: sympathy has critical reservations and criticism has sentimental weaknesses. In *Finnegans Wake*, in spite of the old grudges and the deep scars, Joyce attains—at a stupendous price—a robustious serenity. In security, his writing grows more impersonal; both artist and public are less in evidence.

Joyce's case history, subtly and painstakingly analysed by himself, is the exception to prove the rule that literature cannot exist without an audience. His feeling for an audience is that of the hero of *Exiles* for his wife, when he tells her that she must know him, though he can never know her. Like Mann's *Tonio Kröger*, Joyce can neither live with bourgeois society nor without it. The animus which led him—in 1904, after the day described in *Ulysses*, and again in 1912, after the destruction of the sheets of *Dubliners*—to have scurrilous broadsides printed on the continent, dispatched back to Ireland, and distributed at the doorsteps of his Dublin acquaintances, is writ large in his later work. Through the informal relaxation of *Finnegans Wake*, he presents a masterpiece of self-caricature in the person of his Holiness, the Gripes, who has left the church because the grapes were sour anyway, and who would be pope of a little religion of his own. Belatedly, Stephen performs his Easter duty.

Joyce's self-conscious gestures were inspired by rebellious pride, not by bohemian indifference. He did not want to forget those things he had rebelled against. He wanted, with all the fervour of his ingrown patriotism and perverted piety, with infinite pains and incredible virtuosity, to recreate his own parish at the core of a dedalocentric universe. It is ironic and pitiful that, in pursuance of those aims, he left himself open to attack—from venal and vulgar writers—as an enemy of literary standards. In an irresponsible time, on the contrary, the responsible artist is a lone custodian of tradition. Thus Eliot can be more orthodox than the Lambeth Conference. And Joyce, banished by his fellow-citizens, can retort, with Coriolanus, 'I banish you!' But modern institutions, though they may be slack and unorthodox, exert counter-claims which cannot be lightly rejected. When those two sets of responsibilities, past and present, conflict in the artist's mind, the outcome is neurosis. The artist—under the scrutiny of Freud—is one who, excluded from the substantial satisfactions of life, achieves them by means of fantasy, and, by means of his achievement, finds a pathway back to reality.

Even Flaubert could not stay in the ascetic realm of Saint Anthony. When he died, impenitently hating the *bourgeoisie*, he was compiling an encyclopedia of their opinions and habits—*Bouvard et Pécuchet*, a book which has been compared to *Ulysses* by Ezra Pound. '*Il faut marcher avec son siècle!*' as M. Homais used to say. Joyce, perennially fascinated by the usual, chose the subject of Ulysses because it embodied everything. By crowding in sensory data and cataloguing quotidian items, he hoped to bridge the gap between the self and the *en masse*. Stendhal, throwing himself naïvely into the battle of Waterloo, gives us a fuller realization than Hardy does by contemplating the battlefield from a remote planet. The artistic problem, for either the symbolist or the naturalist, for either Racine or Jane Austen, is to refine observation by selection, to employ the part for the whole. But

Joyce, a transitional artist like Rabelais or Milton, gains his ends by amassing commonplaces. The grandeur of generality, for them, had a baroque design, a simplified outline and an elaborated surface. For Joyce, there will always be a hiatus between the naturalistic texture and the symbolistic structure of his work—a formal reflection of the emotional ambiguity and intellectual equivocation that make him a Janus-faced figure in the history of literature.

The plethora of Joyce's detail is a last exuberant outpouring of naturalism, which has obscured his ultimate importance. He outdid the naturalists at their own game by treating a slice of life so broad and banal that only a myth could lend it shape or meaning. The game he played has been labelled '*Surréalisme*', or superrealism, which is an attempt to push psychological realism to the point of private fantasy. The history of painting would reveal other varieties of post-impressionism, striving toward abstraction not as end in itself, but as a way of clearing the ground for the symbolic frescoes of the future. Joyce's influence has been formidable, rather than encouraging: he has enormously increased the difficulties of being a novelist. He has cleared away the dead lumber of the realistic novel, and invented a whole new arsenal of technical equipment for younger writers. So far, imitation has confined itself to his more superficial traits. John Dos Passos has copied his compound adjectives and tricky mechanics. Thomas Wolfe has taken his example as a licence for unlimited self-absorption. Alfred Döblin and Jules Romains have studied his methods of handling a metropolitan theme. But his style, like Milton's, is more easily parodied than imitated. Like Milton, confident of his eventual authority, he had no disciples.

When Joyce first left Ireland for the continent in 1902, he could hardly have foreseen that the advance of the twentieth century would multiply the phenomenon of the artist as an exile; that the migratory European writer would be no longer the exception but the rule; that the day would come when the story-teller once more —as Mann has poignantly said—would follow a nomadic star. Even when he laboured in Trieste, Zürich, and Paris, from 1914 to 1921, on the most comprehensive record of a city that art has ever undertaken, there was as yet no serious doubt whether the cities of Europe would survive. When he was driven out of France by the German invasion of 1940, and compelled to seek refuge again in the one country of Europe that was still above the battle, he knew the full horror of the nightmare from which he was awakening. It is at these critical points that his life enters history, and his work converges with the main stream of European culture. He began *Ulysses* in 1914, at the beginning of the first World War, and completed *Finnegans Wake* in 1939, at the beginning of the second. Henry James, dying in the second year of the last war, described the world he left as 'a nightmare from which there is no waking save by sleep'. With Joyce's death, in the second year of the present war, a year or two after the deaths of Yeats and Freud and Trotsky, and a month or two before the deaths of Bergson and Virginia Woolf and Frazer, we realize how bare the cultural horizon has become, and how suddenly we are stepping into another age.

When Joyce first set out to write, he defined the double responsibility of the imaginative writer as a task of mediation between the world of reality and the world of dreams. The dissonance between these two worlds, between the imminent realities of the present and the buried dreams of the past, made this task all but impossible. With his other gifts, he brought to it—as Yeats told unresponsive members of the Seanad—'an heroic mind', and completed it by his unexampled devotion. He had, to an unexampled degree, that pride of the creator which is so characteristic of the modern artist, and he likened 'the mystery of esthetic' to the mystery of material creation. Yet it is not within the range of human possibility to create *ex nihilo*. The best writing of our contemporaries is not an act of creation, but an act of evocation, peculiarly saturated with reminiscences. Joyce's imagination evokes the rich stores of memory, which have been the one element of permanence among the many changes of civilization. He reduces past and present to the ageless incantation of the story-teller, the opening words of the *Portrait of the Artist*, 'Once upon a time. . . .' Like the hero of the poem of Yeats, 'He Remembers Forgotten Beauty', he presses in his arms the loveliness which has long ago faded from the world. But Stephen Dedalus, aspiring beyond Michael Robartes, desired to press in his arms 'the loveliness which has not yet come into the world'. When the world has tired of our ugliness and hatred, *Ulysses* will be their monument, and Yeats's lines from 'The Tower' will serve for Joyce's epitaph:

> *I have prepared my peace*
> *With learned Italian things*
> *And the proud stones of Greece,*
> *Poet's imaginings*
> *And memories of love,*
> *Memories of the words of women,*
> *All those things whereof*
> *Man makes a superhuman*
> *Mirror-resembling dream.*

# Revisiting Joyce

'But Truth deals largely with us,' Joyce wrote, in concluding 'The Day of the Rabblement'. Operating posthumously, it has dealt largely with him, justifying his unshakeable confidence in ultimate recognition. Even in the country from which he exiled himself, he is not without honour today. Not that the Irish yet take him seriously, but they are beginning to admire him for having blarneyed the Americans into doing so. Sightseeing tours of Dublin are now conducted, pointing out the Martello Tower where Stephen Dedalus lodged and the pub where Mr. Bloom was insulted. Bloomsday has been officially celebrated by a radio broadcast, which—true to litigious traditions—involved the B.B.C. in a libel suit. On the other hand, members of the Society of Jesus have been thoughtfully studying the works of their wayward pupil. Though Joyce was unsuccessful as a playwright, adaptations from his fiction have lately been enjoying success on the stage: Marjorie Barkentin's *Ulysses in Nighttown* and Mary Manning's *Passages from Finnegans Wake* (New York 1957; in England *The Voice of Shem*, London 1958). The latter source, as Thornton Wilder has freely acknowledged, was likewise the inspiration for his cosmic farce, *The Skin of Our Teeth*. Two of Joyce's letters, begging a loan of forty-five shillings from a publisher who rejected *Dubliners*, according to Padraic Colum, have been auctioned off for thirty pounds. When Professor Peter Allt assumed the chair of English at the University of Groningen in 1952, Joyce was the not inappropriate theme of his inaugural lecture. I have long since lost track of the theses in progress on Joycean subjects.

Merely to enumerate those items of Joyceana which have been

printed since the first edition of the preceding essay would require another and longer book. Two full-length bibliographies are now available: that of Alan Parker (Boston, 1948), which also lists secondary literature, and that of John J. Slocum and Herbert Cahoon (London, 1953), which is authoritative for its listing of Joyce's own work. These guides already need such supplements as James F. Spoerri's news-sheet (University of Virginia Bibliographical Society, October 1955) and the check list of Maurice Beebe and Walton Litz in the Joyce issue of *Modern Fiction Studies* (Spring 1958). A more or less professional quarterly which has been appearing for over two years, *The James Joyce Review*, includes about three hundred titles in its completed bibliography for 1955–57. There has been a *James Joyce Yearbook*, though it limited itself to a single year (1949); and the first *James Joyce Miscellany* of 1957 has just been followed by a second (1959). The average rate of current book publication, so far as a reviewer can estimate, brings no less than a volume a month devoted to some aspect of the man or his work. I cannot pretend to have assimilated all of this material, much less the articles from periodicals. But I have tried to read as I ran, so to speak; and here I shall try to make brief and selective mention of (1) newly published or accessible documents from Joyce's own pen, (2) some of the later biographical and critical writings about him, and (3) trends and counter-trends of interpretation and revaluation.

[i]

'Remember your epiphanies on green oval leaves, deeply deep,' Stephen reminds himself, 'copies to be sent if you died to all the great libraries of the world, including Alexandria.' That reminder has proved to be a prophecy. Not only do the original *Epiphanies* survive in the Lockwood Memorial Library at the University of Buffalo, but most of Joyce's other manuscripts have been finding their way into similar institutions. The British Museum contains the successive drafts of *Finnegans Wake*, very neatly arranged for collation, the gift of Joyce's benefactress and executrix, Harriet

Weaver. Valuable materials are said to have been deposited in the National Library at Dublin, the scene of Stephen's Shakespearean harangue, where they will be discreetly inaccessible for another generation. Several other collections have been established at American universities, largely through the mediation of private collectors and the devotion of Joyce's associates. The Wickser Collection at Buffalo owes its survival to the sacrifice of Paul Léon, his Russian-Jewish friend, who saved it from the Nazis at the cost of his own life. It formed the core of a retrospective exhibition, strikingly set forth in the catalogue of the Librairie La Hune compiled by Bernard Gheerbrant (Paris 1949). The section containing Joyce's personal library has been more precisely catalogued by Thomas E. Connolly (Buffalo 1955). Many of these books are uncut copies inscribed by fellow writers. The volume with the most markings, characteristically, is a confessor's manual in Latin, thereby sustaining our conjecture about the Honuphrius passage in *Finnegans Wake*.

Perhaps the most promising trove of all is the Mennen Collection, most of it obtained via Stanislaus Joyce and recently presented to the Cornell University Library. This, to judge from Arthur Mizener's tantalizing brochure (Ithaca 1958), is especially rich in juvenilia, memorabilia, and correspondence both literary and intimate. Joyce might well have been pleased by the thought that his papers would complete their devious odyssey in a modern Ithaca. Yet, though the curators of such archives are invariably helpful to serious students, and though photographic apparatus has minimized the necessity for travel, one cannot but feel a slight twinge at seeing these *disjecti membra poetae* scattered so profusely across the world. Thus the 383-page fragment acquired in Paris by the Harvard College Library was edited by Theodore Spencer under the title of *Stephen Hero* in 1944. Shortly thereafter at Trieste Mr. Slocum was able to purchase twenty-five additional pages from the same novel, which are now in the Slocum Collection of the Yale University Library, and which—in collaboration with Mr. Cahoon—he added to Spencer's text (Norfolk, Conn., 1955). Now, as if to complicate some twist of Ivy League rivalry, further pages have turned up at Cornell, thereby necessitating a third edition in the near future. Similarly, the student of *Ulysses* will find that the manuscript is in the possession of the Rosenbach Foundation at Philadelphia; but the richest gathering of notes and earlier drafts is at Buffalo, while the page-proofs are privately owned, the galley proofs are at Harvard, and the corrected type-script has been handed out page by page to souvenir-seeking admirers.

However, the disposition of Joyce's effects was bound to reflect the hazards and ironies of his uprooted career. We can imagine him being consoled by the parallel of the several cities that vied in claiming the vagrant Homer after his death. And we can be thankful that so much of the *nachlass* has arrived at a recognized haven somewhere, where it will be securely preserved as part of the extraordinary record. How much remains unpublished which ought to be published is a question for scrupulous appraisal by potential editors and responsible librarians. It would be absurd if Joyce, with all his perfectionism, his endless revisions, and his frequent suppressions, should become a victim of *la fureur de l'inédit*. His mastery of verbal artifice makes it important for critics to scan his notebooks and sketches, to trace the elaborations from draft to draft, and to report those findings back to interested readers. His tendency to draw so deeply and narrowly on his own experience makes it essential for biographers to take advantage of the large body of documentation his letters provide. But, for his contributions to literature, we must still rely on the canon of works that he himself gave to the world, plus those adumbrations and episodes which stand out from the two or three posthumous volumes of his early writing. I shall not comment further on *Stephen Hero*, since I had access to the manuscript while preparing my study, except to suggest that it deserves more discussion than it has received, both for its relation to the *Portrait of the Artist* and for its own considerable merits.

The *Epiphanies* have been brought out by O. A. Silverman in an elegant but all-too-limited edition (Buffalo 1954). Hence they have not yet made their full impression, though the term itself has become a catchword of criticism and has even been appropriated for his own poems by the French experimentalist, Henri Pichette. Twenty-two of these perceptive notations, surviving on white ruled paper rather than green oval leaves, have been put into print; and at least one other has come to light since at Cornell. They can be profitably read as examples of a unique and delicate *genre*, as concrete manifestations of the scholastic *quidditas* or whatness of things, or as realizations of the theory borrowed from Yeats's 'Adoration of the Magi' that a mystical insight may be imparted to wise men in other cities than Bethlehem. Yet it is even more interesting to read them with Joyce's whole development in mind, and to see how they reappear at crucial moments as the nodes of his mature fiction. To cite an unnoted instance, number VI emerges on the second page of the *Portrait of the Artist*. Stephen at six—it is Joyce in his early version—has perpetrated some mischief and is hiding under the table. His protective mother promises that Jim will apologize. If not, their complaining neighbour—Dante in the *Portrait*—says the eagles will pull out his eyes. This traumatic threat provokes the sense of handicap in the vulnerable child; but it is met and matched by his awakening gift. In his head he makes a little rhyme out of the situation:

> Apologise,
> Pull out his eyes,
> Pull out his eyes,
> Apologise.

Already he is a poet, an artist in miniature; and he is anticipating his vocation, his *apologia pro vita sua*. Fifteen of these epiphanies are just such bits of dialogue overheard in his Dublin youth. The 'spiritual manifestation' is perceived through 'the vulgarity of speech or gesture'. But, according to Joyce's definition, it may also be manifested in 'a memorable phase of the mind itself'. The other seven are lyrical rather than dramatic, prose poems inspired by his lonely first years on the continent. Most haunting is number XV, a dream vision of a maternal figure, reproachful yet forgiving. Her final words—'Who has pity for you when you are sad among the strangers? Years and years I loved you when you lay in my womb'

—echo, with a change of tense but not of time, when the ghost of Stephen's mother confronts him in *Ulysses*. The identification, however, is deeper and broader in the epiphany. As 'mother most venerable', it is the Virgin who speaks in the name of the church to its estranged child, and who will always be 'an imaginative influence in the hearts of my children'.

*The Critical Writings of James Joyce* (London, New York, 1959) have been well gathered together by Ellsworth Mason and Richard Ellmann. Much of this casual prose, eked out with occasional verse, is not strictly critical: it comprises three schoolboy themes and the editorial on the foot-and-mouth disease parodied in *Ulysses*, along with Joyce's cavalier book reviews for the *Daily Express* and his Italian articles on Irish affairs translated from *Il piccolo della sera*. There are almost sixty different pieces, spanning a period of more than forty years: from the famous paper on 'Drama and Life' which provoked so intense a discussion in *Stephen Hero* to the pyrotechnical showpiece in Joyce's later manner, 'From a Banned Writer to a Banned Singer'. In his correspondence Joyce declared more than once that he was 'a bad critic'. He was certainly too concentrated upon his own endeavours to be truly catholic in his tastes or objective in his judgements. But, given the importance of these endeavours, his manifestoes compel our respect and his *obiter dicta* lead us back to his considered achievement. A similar value attaches to his working notes for *Exiles*, which have been printed in a new edition of the play, with an introduction by Padraic Colum (London 1952; New York 1951). They link it, even more strongly than I had surmised, with 'The Dead', so that Joyce's rather equivocal drama is redeemed by his most perfect story. Manuscripts for the latter and other stories from *Dubliners* are in the Slocum Collection; studies of them, in comparison with their periodical printings and their definitive versions, will illustrate and illuminate Joyce's developing technique.

I must confess, with great regret, that I have been somewhat disappointed by Stuart Gilbert's selection, *Letters of James Joyce* (London, New York, 1957). Part of that reaction is due to perfunctory editing, part to the fact that Joyce would not adapt himself to the person-to-person medium. He is impressive when he calls Ibsen or Lady Gregory to witness that he is taking a stand, and he is instructive when he is explaining *Ulysses* to Frank Budgen or *Finnegans Wake* to Miss Weaver; but more and more his personality tends, like his ideal creator, to disappear behind his work. There are innumerable other letters extant, particularly in the Mennen Collection, revealing his more informal sides and his intellectual relationships; it is good news that a second volume will be published soon. Meanwhile, something ought to be said about the state of his texts. The only one that has been fully edited, *Chamber Music* (New York 1954), stands in least need of such treatment; and its editor, William York Tindall, has jeopardized his efforts by appending a naïvely Freudian commentary. A variorum text of the *Portrait* is promised by Chester G. Anderson, who has begun by working out a word-index for *Stephen Hero* (Ridgefield, Connecticut, 1958). *Finnegans Wake*, where corrections were inevitable, has been responsibly corrected by its publishers. Not so *Ulysses*; there is a fancy edition with illustrations by Matisse (New York 1935); but the trade editions, both in England and America, persist in *errata*. Incredibly enough, translations have been rendered in many languages, including two in Japanese—a generous requital for Joyce's own translation of Hauptmann into English and of Synge into Italian.

## [ ii ]

Criticism, under its formalistic propulsion of recent years, has tended to look askance at biography. Joyce has therefore confronted it with something of a paradox, since he is both a consummate master of literary form and an inveterate user of autobiographical material. His brother, Stanislaus, uttered a useful caveat when he wrote: '*A Portrait of the Artist* is not an autobiography; it is an artistic creation.' This is well exemplified when Stanislaus, who figures as Maurice in *Stephen Hero*, drops out of the *Portrait*. Nevertheless, James Joyce signed his early stories 'Stephen Daedalus'. Precisely because his career was transmuted into his works, biographical knowledge is a necessary tool for the under-standing of his creative processes. We can consult many witnesses who have given us their memoirs: John Eglinton, Oliver Gogarty, Constantine Curran, Eugene Sheehy for the Dublin days; Arthur Power, Robert McAlmon, Eugene Jolas, Sylvia Beach for Paris; Padraic and Mary Colum for intermittent contacts throughout Joyce's career. We must make due allowance for the axes that are incidentally ground or the egos protected. For example, here is J. F. Byrne, who figures in the *Portrait of the Artist* as Stephen's confidant Cranly, and who has been lately rediscovered living as a retired journalist in Brooklyn. Mr. Byrne's *Silent Years* (New York 1953) is enlightening on a number of Joycean matters, par-ticularly the address of his own family, 7 Eccles Street. But when he goes on to propound an unbreakable cipher, unappreciated by all the military authorities, he incites us to ask ourselves—half a century afterward—which of the two was the fantast, as between the sensible Cranly and the future author of *Finnegans Wake*.

Among these satellites, there is one which has a certain magni-tude of its own, *My Brother's Keeper*, by Stanislaus Joyce (London, New York, 1958). This is not quite what we may have been led to expect, a tale told of Shem by Shaun. Rather, it is the painfully honest testament of an austere and monolithic character, very much more bitter and unbending in his recoil from church and family than his elder brother. To compare the genial warmth of Simon Dedalus with Stanislaus's cold hatred toward their father is to have the measure of James Joyce's sympathies. The gradual passing of his contemporaries has emphasized the need for a biography which would take advantage of first-hand testimony and yet achieve the perspective of objectivity. Herbert Gorman put us all in his debt by working directly with his subject and by printing documents which since have disappeared; but his *James Joyce* was a journalistic piece of writing, and it has dated. Richard Ellmann's forthcoming *James Joyce* will provide us at last with a full-length study of the life and the work in their complex interrelationship. Detailed and comprehensive, candid and judicious, Mr. Ellmann's book may not be completely definitive, since the piles of *inédits* continue to accumulate; but it will put our whole approach to Joyce on a fresh and firm basis. And the emergent personality, with his alcoholic lapses, his financial irresponsibility, the tragedy of his daughter's mental illness, his neurotic obsession with betrayal, his self-centred unconcern with people he could not use, counterweighed by the single-minded exertions of his artistry, will impress and perplex us even more than the embattled artist did in his lifetime.

Glimpses of the younger Joyce in the context of Stephen Dedalus may be gathered from the *Centenary History* of his college debating society, edited by James Meenan (Tralee 1956), which indicates that the paper on drama was better received than its author admitted, and from *The Clongowes Record*, compiled by T. Curran, S.J. (Dublin 1933), which includes photographs of the playing field where Stephen broke his glasses, the long corridor he trod to Father Conmee's study, and that benign cleric himself. The pictorial record has been extended along with Joyce's itinerary, in two attractive albums put together by Patricia Hutchins, from *James Joyce's Dublin* (London 1950) to *James Joyce's World* (London 1957). A pamphlet, *In Memoriam* (Zürich 1941), contains eulogies from Swiss friends on the occasion of Joyce's death; and his final steps have been sympathetically retraced by Leon Edel in *James Joyce: The Last Journey* (New York 1947). The history of Joyce's critical impact is summarized by Marvin Magalaner and Richard M. Kain in *Joyce: The Man, the Work, the Reputation* (New York 1956); but the *Überlieferungsgeschichte* is somewhat blurred by the apparent cross-purposes of the two authors. Many of the best essays—notably those by T. S. Eliot, Edmund Wilson, S. Foster Damon, James T. Farrell, and Philip Toynbee—can be consulted in the convenient anthology of Seon Givens, *James Joyce: Two Decades of Criticism* (New York 1948). Among the other distinguished men of letters who have deposed testimonials, following the precedent of Valery Larbaud, are Hermann Broch, Italo Svevo, Edouard Dujardin, Louis Gillet, Philippe Soupault, Hugh MacDiarmid, Aldous Huxley, and Thornton Wilder. The psychoanalytical monologue of C. G. Jung on *Ulysses* is now obtainable in English translation (Analytical Psychology Club of New York, 1949).

Joycean scholarship has become so highly specialized that we may count at least four volumes on various phases of his concern with religion alone: by Kristian Smidt, William Noon, S.J., Kevin Sullivan, and J. Mitchell Morse. His individual relations with other writers have also been treated on a monographic scale, justifiably when the influence is as central as that of Shakespeare or Aquinas, misleadingly when the connection is as tangential as that of Mallarmé. Because of the problems Joyce has presented to readers, the principal mode of discussion has been what scholars call exegesis—a term which implies that the Scriptures are being interpreted. The pattern was set by Stuart Gilbert's authorized commentary (revised edition 1950), which, besides explaining the classical parallels and esoteric allusions, offered the public a synopsis and sampling at a time when *Ulysses* was forbidden in Britain and America. Many informal sidelights were added by the painter Frank Budgen, out of his friendship with Joyce while *Ulysses* was in the making; these have been supplemented with *Further Recollections* (London 1955). Richard M. Kain, in his *Fabulous Voyager* (Chicago, London, 1947; New York 1959), anchored *Ulysses* solidly to its social environment and made a stronger case than previous commentators for the humanity of Joyce's characters. At this point, the actual sense of the narrative seems to be generally understood; and subsequent interpretations, such as Hugh Kenner's in *Dublin's Joyce* (Bloomington, London 1956), tend to become capricious and doctrinaire through their very effort to discover novel readings. *James Joyce par lui-même* by Jean Paris (Paris 1957) might more aptly have been entitled *Jean Paris par James Joyce*.

In signalizing the dangers of subjective over-reading, I do not mean to suggest that we have wrested the last iota of meaning out of *Ulysses* or that significant researches are not continuing. Experts can still annotate it on technical matters, as Frederick W. Sternfeld has done for its use of music (*English Institute Essays*, 1956). A. M. Klein has commented on specific chapters with Talmudic meticulosity. Joseph Prescott has been reconstructing, with precision and acumen, the process of composition. Thanks to such concrete studies, *Ulysses* is no longer opaque; yet there are those who would restore its opacity, and make it—to paraphrase Haines on Shakespeare—a happy hunting ground for minds that have lost their balance. Whereas *Finnegans Wake*, it must be conceded, virtually invites that kind of response. While *Work in Progress* was being serialized in *transition*, Eugene Jolas and other members of the Joyce coterie heralded it with their *Exagmination* (Paris 1929; London 1936). But after the publication of the *Wake*, there was no opportunity to prepare such an official guide as Mr. Gilbert had supplied for *Ulysses*. The best subterfuge was termed by its collaborators, Joseph Campbell and Henry Morton Robinson, *A Skeleton Key to Finnegans Wake* (London 1947; New York 1944). It effected surreptitious entrance, and subjected the dark interior to a bold, quick flashlight view; but its basic method, a page-by-page attempt to abridge the putative story, was bound to miss more than it caught. Adaline Glasheen's *Census of Finnegans Wake* (London 1957; Evanston 1956), which indexes the characters and roles, affords a more dynamic approach to Joyce's themes and devices.

David Hayman, in the *Publications of the Modern Language Association* (March 1958), devotes some 15,000 words to explicating a single sentence from *Finnegans Wake*, following its elaboration through seventeen drafts, yet scarcely reaching an integrated conception. Furthermore, the article argues, we ought not to look for a core of significance; instead, we should seek our reward in the interplay of particulars. I believe Mr. Hayman may be right, to the extent that we must not expect to crack a code and find everything made luminously clear. We understand the verbal techniques and the underlying ideas fairly well; but each new sentence enmeshes us in its own tangle of peripheral references. These we can untangle sooner or later, if they involve a passage from Quinet or a case-history from Morton Prince or a figment of Hindu mythology or an Edwardian music-hall song. Yet nothing short of telepathy with the dead can reconstitute those chains of personal association which, as we realize more and more, Joyce arbitrarily interwove with his cultural fantasy. It is as if the monument were to remain half-excavated, its outlines roughly marked, its texture admired in fragments, some of its treasures assessed, while the secrets buried with its sardonic artificer went on provoking conjectures and speculations indefinitely. Today there are a number of antiquarian hobbyists who play the game, with resourceful skill, at the level of *Notes and Queries*. But it is twenty years since *Finnegans Wake* was published, and thirty-five years since *Work in Progress* began to appear in print; and I must admit that I am slightly discouraged— not so much by the complexities of the work as by the shortness of human life.

## [ iii ]

To some it may seem amusing to associate Saint Augustine with a hippopotamus because he was Bishop of Hippo. To others it may seem irreverent, irrelevant, or even irritating. Joyce was willing to rest his whole case on one of Augustine's maxims, which bobs to the surface of *Finnegans Wake* in varying malformations: '*Securus iudicat orbis terrarum.*' The untrammelled judgement of the world, in so far as a critical consensus may be attained, has vindicated *Ulysses*, though it remains suspended over the *Wake*. But general acceptance, the change of status from contraband to scripture, has occasioned certain afterthoughts—particularly on the part of those who are faced with the difficult task of writing English prose fiction after *Ulysses*. Undertaking recently to speak for the generation that grew up with the book, V. S. Pritchett announced that it has shrunk from comic epic to crossword puzzle —'and, as such, a major, unrequited European export to the scholar-technicians of the American universities'. Since Mr. Pritchett's 'reassessment' was written for *The New Statesman*, his transatlantic sneer is a standard ploy, best explained by his economic metaphor. English critics, though very free with their personal impressions and moral evaluations, have always tended to shy away from technical analysis; and Mr. Pritchett is true to himself in his distrust of scholarship. I am reluctant to press what is so clearly a sore point with him, and thoroughly disinclined to engage in international trade wars. Indeed, I should welcome his consignment of Joyce's work to this side of the Atlantic, if British letters could afford to lose it.

There should be no argument over the fact that *Ulysses* has been the great road-block in the path of the contemporary novel. This might have meant that we had come to the end of the road, as some critics have been predicting for altogether too long. However, for the seriously creative writer, it seems to mean that the vehicle has been modified or the direction changed. Joyce's influence has been registered in works as different as William Faulkner's *The Sound and the Fury*, Jean-Paul Sartre's *Les chemins de la liberté*, and Samuel Beckett's *Malone* trilogy. He is a standing example for the younger French school that currently produces its *anti-roman*. But it is evident that he has not had much impact upon English novelists. Brought up short by his monumental obstruction, many of them have taken pedestrian detours back to Trollope. There has been a regression of style, a relaxation of structure, an increasingly journalistic dependence upon subject-matter for its own sake. Undoubtedly, there is a future for the conventional novelist—or a comfortable present rather, safely guaranteed by the circulating libraries and the film rights. But it must be obtained by coming to terms with that 'rabblement' which Joyce repudiated from the beginning of his career, and whose 'mean influences' are so much more effective and subtle today. 'In reading Joyce,' Frank O'Connor complains, 'one is reading Literature—Literature with a capital L.' We need not disagree; we need merely recognize the sharp decline in literary standards that could make such an assertion an accusation. 'Gawd damn it,' wrote Ezra Pound to Joyce in his first enthusiasm over *Ulysses*, 'it is Writing, with a large W and no C.'

Flaubert, who was also guilty of practising literature with a capital L, and who is therefore included in Mr. O'Connor's indictment, frankly chose to regard himself as a mandarin. The epithet, in its splendour and misery, might well be applied to Joyce. Both men were writers' writers, ambitious proponents of the word at its most expressive, painstaking votaries of what André Malraux has called the religion of art. It was much harder to live up to that creed for an exiled Irishman in the early twentieth century than it had been for a French recluse in the mid-nineteenth, and it is probable that we have witnessed the passing of the order they both represent: the *modus vivendi* of the passionately dedicated, extravagantly learned, rigorously detached intellectual. But it should be no cause for satisfaction to pass from a mandarin culture into a culture for coolies; and if the Flaubertian or Joycean virtues can no longer be cultivated, that is no reason for ceasing to admire them. Mr. O'Connor is a pleasant purveyor of literature in the lower case, an easy-going Irish raconteur whose entire output is derived from the vein of the simpler stories in *Dubliners*. One can see how he might be made uneasy by the way in which Joyce moved on from *Dubliners* to the *Portrait of the Artist*, from the *Portrait* to *Ulysses*, and from *Ulysses* to *Finnegans Wake*. Such has distinctively been the way of the modernist; and as modernism recedes into the background, as we settle down into what Arnold Toynbee would classify as the post-modern period, Joyce assumes a predominating position in any retrospect of the moderns in English.

We should remember or we should try to recapture the overtones of the date attached to his first published essay, his self-identification with Ibsen's iconoclasm, and to his defence of what he designated as 'the New School' before his college debating society. 1900! To have been alive and young then must have seemed peculiarly blissful. Joyce was eighteen; he had spent his adolescence in the *fin du siècle*, the years of self-conscious artistic decadence; and then—it must have been sudden and striking—had entered the twentieth century, the age of science, novelty, and promise. Like his gifted contemporaries who were youths in the eighteen-nineties and reached their prime in the nineteen-twenties, Eliot in poetry, Stravinsky in music, Picasso in painting, he could look both ways: backward toward the accumulated riches of tradition and forward toward the untold possibilities of experiment. Like those other modernists, he could emulate the schools and styles of other periods; like them, he had a restless impulse to outdo himself by moving on from one inventive mood to another. This may help to explain the ups and downs of his reception, and his quick transit from the *avant-garde* to the academy. When Thomas Merton, the loquacious Trappist, testifies that Joyce's writings aided in his conversion to Catholicism, it is a far cry from the shocks and scandals that they so often elicited during the 'twenties. Joyce's own progression from naturalist to symbolist has been a perspicuous sign of the changing times. The youthful sense of immediacy, of going forth to encounter the reality of experience, yielded to withdrawal, indirection, and remote contemplation.

For his original readers Joyce was a heretic, for many of them an emancipating force. The shift of values at mid-century has recast him in a priestly role, the patriarch of a neo-orthodox cult. He had lent himself to this reorientation by shifting his ground from Icarian revolt to Daedalean wordplay. Gradually, George Orwell has severely but justly remarked, the novelist had been smothered by the lexicographer. But Stephen Dedalus knew where he was heading, when he planned to send his manuscripts to all the libraries of the world, including Alexandria; for Alexandrianism, with its self-conscious bookishness, stood as a kind of outpost against barbarianism. Its museum-like state of mind may be our only alternative to the mental climate that surrounds our mundane lives, the standardized vulgarity that seeps through the minds of Bloom and Earwicker, the effects of 'Pop Kulch' that Joyce so acutely discerned, even before electronics had amplified them. Consequently it does not seem far-fetched, though it may well be regrettable, to see him handed over to the scholiasts, the doctoral candidates, and the academic disciples; inasmuch as it is their business to master the arts of language, they could hardly have found a better model. Nor is it finally surprising that he, who so expressly resisted a professorial chair, should attract the keenest interest of students and be most highly valued in universities. We are likely to remember him best as a student, fervently discussing

Yeats with his classmates at the National Library, or walking across the portico of the Museum and looking toward the sky for an augury.

That is the location for the bookish episode of *Ulysses*, where Stephen holds forth on Shakespeare. The occasion is his farewell to the leading lights of the Irish renascence. The scene is set by the books on the walls, with their accumulations of dead learning, 'coffined thoughts about me in mummycases, embalmed in spice of words'. As he speaks, he silently invokes the mythical inventor of writing, the thrice-great Hermes of the Egyptians, 'Thoth, god of libraries'. But John Eglinton is not impressed enough to commission an article; and Æ pontificates: 'Our national epic has yet to be written.' So Stephen leaves with Mulligan, walking through the turnstile and along the colonnade, scarcely noticing the shabby stranger—so ill at ease in that hermetic sanctuary—who will become the hero of Joyce's national epic, Leopold Bloom. Their recognition scene will take place later, significantly in the street. Earlier that day, Stephen has taken leave of his job as a schoolmaster.

—I foresee, Mr. Deasy said, that you will not remain here very long at this work. You were not born to be a teacher, I think. Perhaps I am wrong.

—A learner rather, Stephen said.

And here what will you learn more?

Mr Deasy shook his head.

—Who knows? he said. To learn one must be humble. But life is the great teacher.

How trite, how true! And the great writer is one who can teach us those lessons which he has, so often painfully, learned from life. What, then, did Joyce learn from the postgraduate course he took by leaving Dublin for the continent? The answer, I think, is suggested by Stephen's mother. In the concluding pages of the *Portrait*, he records his last discussions with her before his first departure. Some of them were arguments: 'Subject: B. V. M.' The Blessed Virgin Mary, mother most venerable, venerated so ardently in his school days, will blend with the matriarchal figure of May Dedalus, in revisiting Stephen when he is sad among the strangers. The penultimate entry in Stephen's journal is frequently cited for its flourish about 'the uncreated conscience of my race'. Less well remembered is her appeal to his conscience, while she is maternally packing his clothes: 'She prays now, she says, that I may learn in my own life and away from home and friends what the heart is and what it feels.' Could we not conclude, in all reverence, that *Ulysses* answered that prayer? Joyce was so much the scholar and technician that, in my own pedagogical effort on his behalf, I may have under-emphasized such a conclusion. May I now say that the Joyce for whom I would bespeak your continued admiration is the learner and teacher?

# Index

# Index

# Index

# Index

# Index

# Index